Macmillan Computer Science Series

£13.99
3C96

Consul

A. Abdel Dahman and M. Limame, *C a sort's guide*
Ian O. Angell, *High-resolution Computer Graphics Using C*
Ian O. Angell and Gareth Griffith, *High-resolution Computer Graphics Using FORTRAN 77*
Ian O. Angell and Gareth Griffith, *High-resolution Computer Graphics Using Pascal*
M. Azmoodeh, *Abstract Data Types and Algorithms, second edition*
C. Bamford and P. Curran, *Data Structures, Files and Databases, second edition*
P. Beynon-Davies, *Information Systems Development, second edition*
G.M. Birtwistle, *Discrete Event Modelling on Simula*
Linda E.M. Brackenbury, *Design of VLSI Systems – A Practical Introduction*
Alan Bradley, *Peripherals for Computer Systems*
G.R. Brookes and A.J. Stewart, *Introduction to occam 2 on the Transputer*
P.C. Capon and P.J. Jinks, *Compiler Engineering Using Pascal*
Robert Cole, *Computer Communications, second edition*
E. Davalo and P. Naïm, *Neural Networks*
S.M. Deen, *Principles and Practice of Database Systems*
D. England *et al.*, *A Sun User's Guide, second edition*
Jean Ettinger, *Programming in C++*
J.S. Florentin, *Microprogrammed Systems Design*
A.B. Fontaine and F. Barrand, *80286 and 80386 Microprocessors*
Michel Gauthier, *Ada – A Professional Course*
M.G. Hartley, M. Healey and P.G. Depledge, *Mini and Microcomputer Systems*
J.A. Hewitt and R.J. Frank, *Software Engineering in Modula-2 – An Object-oriented Approach*
M.J. King and J.P. Pardoe, *Program Design Using JSP – A Practical Introduction, second edition*
Bernard Leguy, *Ada – A Programmer's Introduction*
M. Léonard, *Database Design Theory*
David Lightfoot, *Formal Specification Using Z*
A.M. Lister and R.D. Eager, *Fundamentals of Operating Systems, fifth edition*
Elizabeth Lynch, *Understanding SQL*
B. A. E. Meekings, T. P. Kudrycki and M. D. Soren, *A Book on C, third edition*
R. J. Mitchell, *C++ Object-Oriented Programming*
R.J. Mitchell, *Microcomputer Systems Using the STE Bus*
R.J. Mitchell, *Modula-2 Applied*
Y. Nishinuma and R. Espesser, *UNIX – First Contact*
Pham Thu Quang and C. Chartier-Kastler, *MERISE in Practice*

Continued overleaf

Macmillan Computer Science Series (continued)

Ian Pratt, *Artificial Intelligence*
E.J. Redfern, *Introduction to Pascal for Computational Mathematics*
Gordon Reece, *Microcomputer Modelling by Finite Differences*
F. D. Rolland, *Programming with VDM*
L.E. Scales, *Introduction to Non-Linear Optimization*
A.G. Sutcliffe, *Human–Computer Interface Design, second edition*
Colin J. Theaker and Graham R. Brookes, *Concepts of Operating Systems*
M. Thorin, *Real-time Transaction Processing*
M.R. Tolhurst *et al.*, *Open Systems Interconnection*

Non-series

I.O. Angell and D. Tsoubelis, *Advanced Graphics on VGA and XGA Cards using Borland C++*
N. Frude, *A Guide to SPSS/PC+, second edition*
Percy Mett, *Introduction to Computing*
Tony Royce, *COBOL – An Introduction*
Tony Royce, *Structured COBOL – An Introduction*
Tony Royce, *C Programming – An Introduction*

Program Design Using JSP
A Practical Introduction

M. J. King and J. P. Pardoe

School of Computing and Mathematical Sciences
Liverpool John Moore's University

Second Edition

MACMILLAN

First edition 1985
Second edition 1992

Published by
MACMILLAN PRESS LTD
Houndmills, Basingstoke, Hampshire RG21 6XS
and London
Companies and representatives
throughout the world

ISBN 0–333–57673–X hardcover
ISBN 0–333–57674–8 paperback

A catalogue record for this book is available
from the British Library.

12 11 10   9   8   7   6   5   4
03 02 01 00 99 98 97 96 95

Printed and bound in Great Britain by
Antony Rowe Ltd, Chippenham, Wiltshire

Contents

Preface

Aims of the book

This text aims to provide a practical course for those who want to both understand and apply the Jackson Structured Programming (JSP) approach to program design. It has been designed for trainee and experienced programmers, and students on BTEC courses (such as the Higher National Diploma in Computing) and degree courses that incorporate the study of program design.

The aim is to present the principles and techniques of JSP in a way that will enable the reader to apply the method with confidence.

Structure of the book

The book first presents, in chapters 1-6, the basic method for relatively straightforward problems while stressing the important aspects through numerous examples and exercises. The production of logical data structures, being the basis of the method and the area where students may initially encounter difficulties, is dealt with at length. Chapter 4 then explains how the identification of corresponding components in the input and output structures enables them to be combined to form a program structure. The allocation of conditions and operations to this program structure is covered in chapter 5; conversion of the program structure with allocated conditions and operations into schematic logic (that is, a pseudo-code representation) is then explained in chapter 6.

Since JSP does not presume upon any particular programming language, neither does this book. However, to illustrate the ease with which programs can be coded after they have been designed in a language-free manner, the appropriate coding rules for COBOL and Pascal are outlined in chapter 7.

After the basic techniques have been mastered, the student may then proceed to the more difficult aspects. The concepts of processing more than one input file, including different types of merge problems, are examined in detail. The concepts of structure clashes and recognition problems, together with their solutions (that is, inversion and backtracking respectively) are examined in a practical manner. Interactive programs appear to be a special class of problem, so a separate chapter deals with the application of the method to such problems.

The book also illustrates the usefulness of the design method in respect of procedurisation, testing, documentation and amendment of existing programs. Special attention is given to a structural testing method.

Use of the book

To ensure that each technique is mastered as it is introduced, we strongly urge the reader to attempt all the exercises given at the end of most chapters, and to arrive at his/her own solutions before turning to the solutions provided in appendix A.

Since this is primarily a book on program design, these solutions are normally given as logical data structures, program structure diagrams with allocated conditions and operations, or as schematic logic. However, having completed the design, the reader may wish to experience the satisfaction of running the program by translating certain solutions into a target language (see chapter 7).

Four case studies and their solutions are also provided in the appendixes. A note is included at the end of chapters 6, 9, 10 and 12, indicating that the appropriate case study may then be attempted. These extended problems can therefore be used for reinforcement and additional practice immediately after the appropriate chapter, or for revision purposes at a later stage.

Acknowledgements

It would be inappropriate to write a book on JSP without acknowledging the work of Michael Jackson, particularly his book *Principles of Program Design*. Our interest in Jackson's method was also stimulated by Brian Ratcliff of the Universtity of Aston in Birmingham.

We would like to thank our colleagues at Liverpool Polytechnic for their advice, assistance and encouragement. Our thanks also to all those students who attended the lecture courses on which this book is based - their questions and comments have helped enormously and contributed to the changes made in this second edition.

1 The Importance of Program Design

1.1 Introduction

The importance of properly designed software of any kind, from the trivial application program to the most complex operating system, cannot be over-stressed. In these days when software production and maintenance costs are escalating in relation to total system costs and there is a shortage of skilled software producers, the computing profession can ill-afford to produce substandard software. Yet, much poor software is produced, mainly due to poor problem definition and poor program design.

Much can be done to improve problem definition, and the problem of poor program design can be overcome by the adoption of formalised methods of design.

To quote Wirth [*Communications of the ACM*, April 1971, p.221] 'Programming courses should teach methods of design and construction, and the selected examples should be such that a gradual development can be nicely demonstrated.'

This text aims to satisfy these criteria by concentrating on a particular design method, namely Jackson Structured Programming (JSP). In this chapter, we discuss briefly the general requirements of a software design method and provide an overview of JSP.

1.2 Requirements of a software design method

A software design method is a set of basic principles and techniques that enables problems to be solved using a computer. Any design method worth using must have a set of rules to identify the class of problem that can be solved and to guide the problem solver in a step-by-step manner through the various stages of software production. It must emphasise that the solution of the problem is dependent on the transformation of the input data into results. The outcome of each stage in the design process should yield good documentation, allow progress to be assessed and give an early warning of errors. It is critically important that errors are diagnosed as early as possible before they become entrenched and consequently more difficult, and thus more costly, to remove.

1

The requirements of a software design method may be summarised as follows:

1. To enable correct programs to be produced.
2. To facilitate the organised control of software projects.
3. To facilitate the handling of large and/or complex projects.
4. To enable systematic methods to be applied rigorously by trained personnel.
5. To provide a method that is 'workable' within the intellectual limitations of the average programmer.
6. To afford techniques that can be taught and do not rely on inspiration or perspiration.

1.3 The characteristics of JSP

Jackson describes his own method as having the following characteristics:

1. It is non-inspirational; it depends little, or not at all, on invention and insight on the part of the designer.
2. It is rational; the design procedure is based on reasoned principles, and each step may be validated in the light of these principles.
3. It is teachable; people can be taught to practise the method and two or more programmers using the method to solve the same problem will arrive at substantially the same solution.
4. It is practical; the method itself is simple and easy to understand and the designs produced can be implemented without difficulty in any ordinary programming environment.

1.4 The stages of JSP

The details of JSP are developed gradually throughout the book. In this section we merely describe the basic principles and design stages so that the reader may gain some insight into where each stage fits within the overall method.

The principles of JSP are as follows:

1. Analysis of the problem that the program is to solve and the production of structure diagrams; data are usually the basis of the program, so data structures are created.
2. Analysis of the main programming tasks and the production of a program structure based on the data structures.

3. Definition of the tasks in terms of elementary operations and allocation of each of these to the component parts of the program structure.
4. Conversion (or translation) of the program structure and (allocated) operations into a computer programming language.

Specifically, to design a computer program we must:

1. Draw structure diagrams for each set of data such that the structures reflect the way in which the data are to be processed; we may call these 'logical data structures' to distinguish them from 'physical data structures' which take no account of the problem at hand.
2. Identify points of correspondence of a one-for-one nature between components of individual data structures.
3. Produce a program structure diagram using the same notation as for the data structures and based upon the data structures, by combining them at the points of correspondence.
4. Where a single program structure cannot be produced directly from the data structures because of a 'structure clash', proceed to design two (or more) separate programs with communication via an intermediate file which corresponds to both program structures.
5. For each iteration and selection, construct appropriate conditions; where this is not possible use special techniques which overcome recognition problems.
6. Examine the specification and the conditions and from these draw up a list of basic program operations in plain language.
7. Allocate the conditions and operations to the appropriate components of the program structure.
8. Produce 'schematic logic' (pseudo code) from the program structure.
9. Implement the schematic logic in a target high level programming language.

2 Data Structures

2.1 The JSP notation

For any programming problem (not involving parallel activities) structure diagrams may be drawn consisting of just 3 basic construct types:

- ❑ Sequence
- ❑ Iteration (loop)
- ❑ Selection (choice)

(a) The notation for a sequence is shown in figure 2.1.

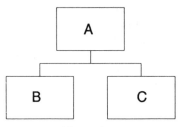

Figure 2.1

Component (box) A is a sequence. Boxes B and C represent component parts of the sequence. In this case they are not further defined and hence have no 'structure' of their own; they are known as elementary components.

In the above example, A is a sequence of the two components B followed by C. The notation could of course be extended for a sequence of any number of component parts.

(b) The notation for an iteration is shown in figure 2.2.

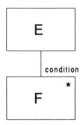

Figure 2.2

Component (box) E is an iteration. The box F is the iteration component part. E is an iteration of a number (possibly zero) of Fs. The number of Fs is controlled by the specified condition.

(c) The notation for a selection is shown in figure 2.3.

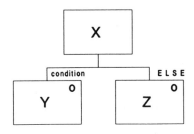

Figure 2.3

Box X is a selection. Boxes Y and Z are component parts of the selection.

In the above example, X is a selection (or choice) of Y or Z. Only the condition for the choice of Y is specified - if this condition is not true Z is chosen.

As for a sequence, the notation can be extended for any number of component parts (or choices). The final choice is always governed by the 'else' situation.

For every structure diagram, each component is of a unique type, that is, either a selection or an iteration or a sequence or an elementary component. In drawing a diagram, the type of a particular component is indicated in its component part(s). Thus, when interpreting a structure diagram, the type of a component is deduced by looking at the next level down. In (b) above, for example, we look at the '*' notation in the Box F to deduce that E is an iteration. Similarly, we can see that A is a sequence and X is a selection.

Notice that a component cannot have a mixture of component parts; for example, an iteration may only have one iteration component part, and a selection may only have selection component parts. Figures 2.4 and 2.5 illustrate **incorrect constructs**.

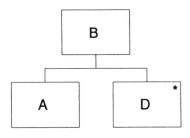

Figure 2.4

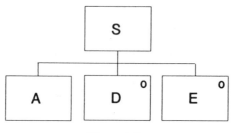

Figure 2.5

In figure 2.4, component B is neither a sequence nor an iteration. In figure 2.5, component S is neither a sequence nor a selection.

2.2 Data and procedures

Structure diagrams can be used to depict data and problem procedures. We will use simple COBOL statements to make this point.

Consider the sequence in section 2.1
procedure:

```
A.
     B.    MOVE 1 TO COUNT.
     C.    ADD 2 TO TOTAL.
```

The procedural component A is a sequence of the component (or statement) labelled B followed by the component (statement) labelled C.
data:

```
01  A.
     03 B     PIC 9.
     03 C     PIC X(4).
```

The data component (record) A is a sequence of the component (or field) B followed by the component (field) C.

Consider the iteration in section 2.1
procedure:

```
E.
          PERFORM F UNTIL CONDITION-1.
```

The procedural component E is an iteration (or repetition) of the component F until some terminating condition.
data:

```
01  E.
     03 F     PIC X(4) OCCURS N TIMES.
```

The data component (record) E is an iteration (or repetition) of the data component (or field) labelled F. That is, E contains N occurrences of F.

Finally, consider the selection in section 2.1
procedure:

```
X.
    IF CONDITION-FOR-Y
        PERFORM Y
    ELSE
        PERFORM Z.
```

The procedural component X executes a selection of either the component Y or the component Z depending upon the stated condition.
data:

```
01  X.
    03 Y    PIC X(4).
    03 Z    REDEFINES Y PIC 9(4).
```

The data component X is a selection of either the component (field) Y which has one definition, or the component (field) Z which has another definition.

2.3 Examples of how data structures are produced

When developing data structures, we strongly recommend the following approach, particularly the use of an annotated sketch, for all but the most trivial cases.

1. From the given narrative, first note the smallest data items of interest, then sketch sample data in a form that clearly indicates all relevant features including any repetitions (as these will become iteration component parts) and choices (as these will become selection component parts).
2. Working from the top level down to the smallest required data item, and for each level in turn, identify relevant groupings and ordering of the data, clearly indicating any repetitions and selections.
3. Translate this annotated sketch into a structure diagram.
4. Verify your structure diagram by reading it back to yourself checking that it is consistent with and incorporates all features of the given narrative.

Notice that each representation of the data, the given narrative, the annotated sketch with groupings and the structure diagram, is in effect a different way of communicating the same information.

The following examples show how a data structure may be produced from a narrative description using the three constructs, described in section 2.1, in various combinations.

(a) Consider a pack of playing cards as data. If the cards are not sorted the data can be represented by the annotated sketch shown as figure

2.6. Note the use of the same code (CD) to identify each component part of the iteration, that is, the repeated data items. This can now be easily translated into the data structure given as figure 2.7.

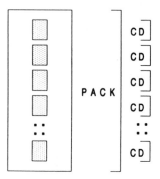

Figure 2.6

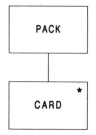

Figure 2.7

At this stage we do not include conditions on the structure diagram. However, there is no harm in considering what the condition should be. In this case, it is obviously UNTIL END OF PACK.

(b) If the pack was sorted by suit, all the spades, then the hearts, then the diamonds, then the clubs, we would need to show this division of suits and the order of their appearance in the pack. Figure 2.8 is an annotated sketch that will help you to visualise the structure. From the sketch, we see that the PACK is now a sequence of SPADE SUIT, then HEART SUIT, then DIAMOND SUIT, then CLUB SUIT. Each suit is then an iteration of the appropriate card type. From this sketch we arrive at the data structure given in figure 2.9.

(c) Again, consider a complete pack of playing cards with just the first card face up. If it is a picture card we win, otherwise we lose. An annotated sketch is given as figure 2.10, and the data structure for

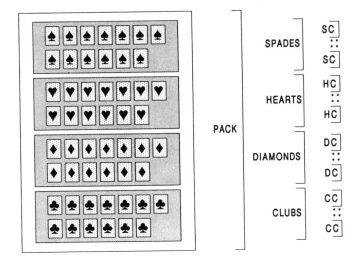

Figure 2.8

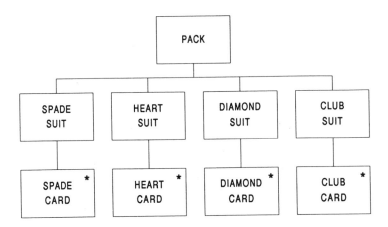

Figure 2.9

the pack is shown in figure 2.11. In this case, although we have shown the remainder of the pack as an iteration of 51 occurrences of card it is really irrelevant to the problem we are trying to depict. If we chose to omit this detail we would be making a distinction between the physical structure of the pack of cards and the logical structure in respect of the problem being tackled. We shall consider this distinction in the next chapter.

(d) In a game of 5 card poker, two hands are left in the game. Honest

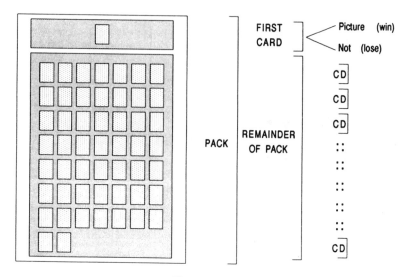

Figure 2.10

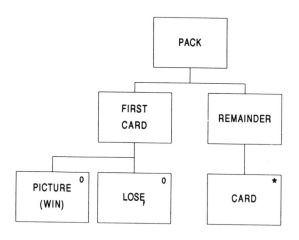

Figure 2.11

Joe has three aces and two kings. Dodgy George, therefore, has a hand of cards which may either win or lose. To win he must have a running flush or four of a kind. In this case, sketching the data for George's hand is no real help. We simply need to recognise that the hand is either a winner or a loser, that there are two possible ways of winning and that each possible hand is an iteration of card. The structure diagram is given as figure 2.12.

Notice that in this example we have a selection where one of the

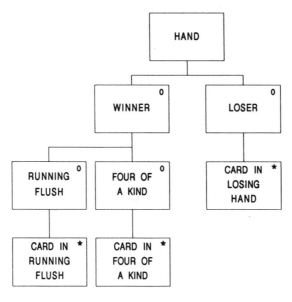

Figure 2.12

selected components is itself a selection. In such cases we may consider combining these selections at one level, giving HAND as a selection of the three components WINNER WITH RUNNING FLUSH or WINNER WITH FOUR OF A KIND or LOSER. You might care to draw this alternative structure and consider which if any is better.

(e) Let us now consider a computer file. A sales file contains a header record, followed by detail records grouped according to the month, with a total at the end of each month. At the end of the file there may or may not be a grand total record.

We note that a record is the smallest item of interest and then list a typical sales file with one record per line. (Notice that we have omitted some of the repeated groups but indicated their omission by dotted lines.) We then identify the order and grouping of the data by working from the top level and considering each level in turn. The resultant annotated sketch is shown as figure 2.13.

We perceive, at the top level, that the SALES FILE consists of three parts - the HEADER RECORD (HR) followed by the SALES FILE BODY and then the GRAND TOTAL RECORD (GTR). It is therefore a sequence.

Now consider the next level. HEADER RECORD needs no further refinement and from the narrative we know that GRAND TOTAL RECORD is a selection with elementary component parts; SALES FILE BODY is an iteration of MONTHLY SECTION.

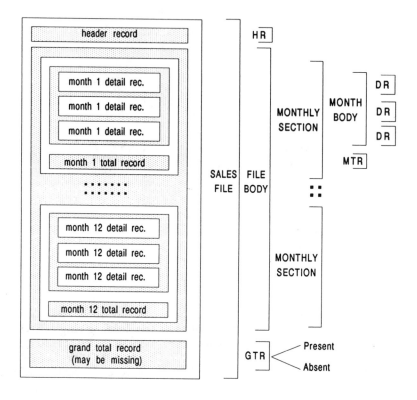

Figure 2.13

Concentrating on MONTHLY SECTION reveals a sequence of MONTHLY SECTION BODY followed by MONTH TOTAL RECORD (MTR).

Finally MONTHLY SECTION BODY is an iteration of DETAIL RECORD (DR). Thus, the data structure is as shown in figure 2.14.

When considering later examples or attempting exercises, we strongly recommend the use of an annotated sketch similar to figure 2.13. You may wish to devise your own notation, but note the repeated use of the same nomenclature (for example, MONTHLY SECTION and DR) to identify the component part of an iteration.

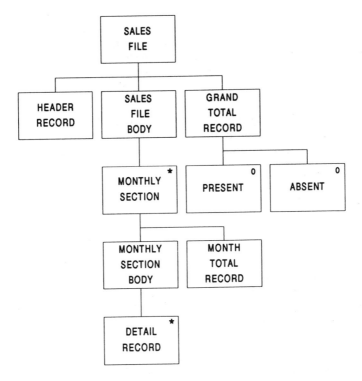

Figure 2.14

2.4 Exercises

2.4.1 Suppose the pack of cards was arranged such that we have all the picture cards first, followed by the rest of the pack. What would be an appropriate data structure? Produce an annotated sketch of the data before drawing the data structure.

2.4.2 From a shuffled pack, you deal a hand face upwards until you have dealt an ace. Produce an annotated sketch of the hand that you have dealt. Then draw a data structure diagram. What is the minimum number of cards in the hand?

2.4.3 The pack of cards is sorted by suit, but the order of the suits is not known. Produce an annotated sketch of some data, then draw a data structure diagram.

2.4.4   A book consists of a number of chapters followed by an appendix. Each chapter consists of a number of paragraphs and the appendix has a number of keyword sections consisting of one or more definitions. Produce an annotated sketch·of some data, then draw the data structure.

2.4.5   A customer file is sorted by region code. There are a number of regions in the file and there could be any number of records per region. Produce an annotated sketch of a sample file, then draw the data structure.

2.4.6   The same customer file is sorted by credit limit code within region code. Produce an annotated sketch of a sample file, then draw the data structure.

2.4.7   An invoice has the customer's name and address at the top and the total amount payable at the bottom. In between there are a number of lines for individual items (we may call this the body of the invoice). Produce an annotated sketch of a sample invoice, then draw the data structure.

2.4.8   A fence consists of a number of posts each followed by 10 boards, and then a final post at the end, as shown in figure 2.15. Identify the ordered components and the groupings in figure 2.15, then draw a data structure diagram for the fence.

Figure 2.15

2.4.9   Amend the above for a fence where the last section has only 6 boards.

2.4.10   The standard design for a house includes a specification as follows. The front of the house (looking at it from left to right) has a large window which may be Georgian style or a picture window, followed by a door which may or may not have a glazed upper section. If the door has no glazing it may be painted red or green; glazed doors are always green. After the door (on the right-hand side of the house) there are either two small windows or a large window. Draw an annotated sketch and a data structure for the front of the house.

2.4.11 In a 'fun run' a majority of the runners completed the course and of these a significant proportion recorded their best time. There was no discrimination between the sexes, but there were two categories of runner - 'beginner' and 'past-it'. Draw an annotated sketch and data structure of all the competitors using the above information.

For this problem it is necessary to think in terms of the different choices in describing a runner. For example, a runner may or may not complete the course. Whether he completes the course or not, he may or may not be a beginner. If he completes the course, he may or may not achieve a personal best time. Hence the solution does not reflect the order in which the competitors finished, but shows the different ways in which a runner can be described as a number of related selections.

2.4.12 A disk contains production details as follows. For each machine group there are a number of detailed records followed by a total record; for each area there are a number of machine groups. At the end of the file there may or may not be a grand total record. Produce an annotated sketch of a sample production file, then draw the data structure.

3 Data Structures for Particular Problems

3.1 Physical data structures and logical data structures

A physical data structure fully describes some data without taking into account any particular use to which the data may be put; that is, without taking into account the problem under consideration.

A logical data structure describes some data in respect of a particular use or for a certain problem. For example, the physical data structure of a pack of playing cards which are fully sorted (ace to king) for each suit, but with no particular suit order, is shown in figure 3.1.

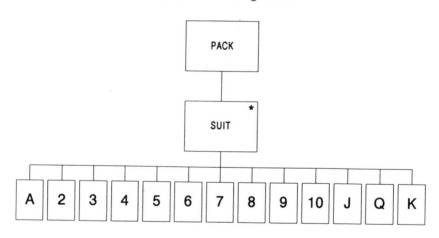

Figure 3.1

A logical data structure cannot deny any of the components of the physical structure and is essentially an extract of it. For example, given the same pack of cards, but with a problem specification of isolating the aces, we would draw the logical data structure shown in figure 3.2.

Given the same sorted pack of cards, let us now consider the problem of putting all of the hearts on the right hand side of the table and all of the cards in the other suits on the left hand side. The logical data structure represents how we would 'view' or 'process' the data for that particular

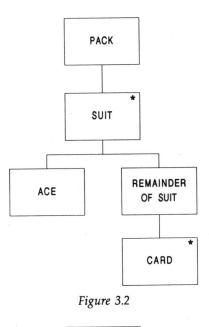

Figure 3.2

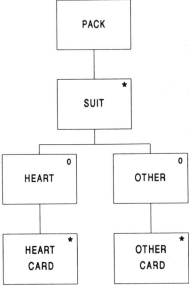

Figure 3.3

problem. This data structure is shown in figure 3.3.

It is stressed that, although the physical data structure remains un-
altered, we may arrive at different logical structures depending on the
problem. The logical structures must always be consistent with the physical

data structure; that is, they must not violate the physical structure. You should convince yourself that this is true in the above example.

3.2 A logical data structure for a simple problem

Let us now consider certain aspects of logical data structures in the context of producing a program. Eventually, we shall draw logical data structures for all input and output files, combine these to produce a program structure and then allocate conditions and operations (e.g. print report headings) which can easily be translated into a programming language. At this stage, we are concentrating on the production of individual logical data structures, which reflect the structure and processing logic of the problem.

A file containing records of students on a three-year course is sorted into ascending order of year. A program is required to count the number of second-year students who have paid their fees. A sketch of a typical file showing its logical groupings and emphasising the order of its components is given in figure 3.4. Noting that the component SECOND YEAR contains data items indicating either 'paid fees' or 'not paid', that is, a selection, we can produce the logical data structure as shown in figure 3.5.

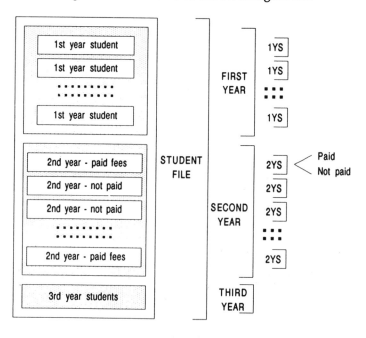

Figure 3.4

Note that figure 3.5 reflects the way in which the data are to be processed, but does not contain any processing detail such as 'read student

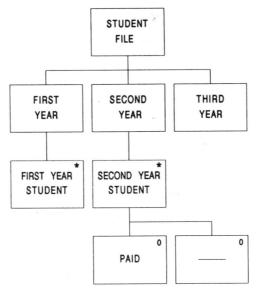

Figure 3.5

file' or 'increment student-paid count'.

Output from the program would contain, amongst other things, the required student total, but this element of data does not appear on the input file and therefore does not appear on the above structure.

The selection SECOND YEAR STUDENT is necessary because the way in which we are to process a second-year student depends on whether the appropriate data on the student record indicates payment of fees or not. We have introduced here the null elementary component (the selection part with a dash in) which may be used for the ELSE option for elementary components.

The component FIRST YEAR is regarded as an iteration of FIRST YEAR STUDENT because we will have to process these records by reading past them. Although the physical data structure would indicate that THIRD YEAR is also an iteration of student, these records do not need to appear on the logical data structure. Omitting this component is allowed in the sense that we are not contradicting the physical structure. However, if a different problem required us to process all the third year students before the first-year students, then we would not be able to draw a logical data structure consistent with the physical organisation.

Since the logical data structure is a representation of 'how' we would process the data for a particular problem, the following illustration may help you to understand how we arrive at this correct structure for the above example. Imagine the student file of records to be a box-file of cards. Just as a computer program has to read one record at a time from the beginning of the file, you flick through the cards from the beginning of the box-file. In this case, you would simply flick through each first-year student card (all year one students are processed the same), then as you go through the second-year student cards, you would note whether or not they have paid their fees (a selection). When you reach the first third year student card, you would stop flicking through the cards, ignoring all cards from this point.

The technique of sketching some sample data and using an approach similar to that outlined above to determine how the data would be processed (in order to identify appropriate groupings, repetitions and selections) can be used to develop a logical data structure for any input file. The processing involved in producing an output file is the actual writing or printing to the file. Thus, the logical data structure for an output file represents what physically appears on the file. As such, the production of logical data structures for output files tends to be somewhat easier than for input files. We would still recommend the use of an annotated sketch, but this will be generally easier to produce and annotate.

3.3 Exercises

Note that each of the first two questions is concerned with an output file. The rest of the exercises refer to input files. Notice also the important points illustrated by exercises 3.3.3, 3.3.4, 3.3.5 and 3.3.6.

3.3.1   A report is to be produced. Each page contains 42 detail lines in addition to page headings and a total line. The total line includes appropriate text, indicating that it may be a grand total or a cumulative carried forward total. Produce a sketch of a sample report, annotate it, then draw the logical data structure for the report file.

3.3.2   Produce an annotated sketch and then the logical data structure for a file of self-adhesive labels where the labels are '3 up' across the page. The labels may contain 3 or 4 lines of print. You may assume that a row of labels can be constructed in memory and that a complete row can be printed before moving on to the next one. This means that you can consider a row as a component containing a number of labels (in this case 3), each of which may contain 3 or 4 lines.

3.3.3   A file contains three different types of records (type 1, type 2, type 3). Records of type 1 are processed by summing the amounts. Records of type 2 are processed according to a region code - if the code is A the record is displayed, otherwise the first 20 characters only are displayed. Records of type 3 are ignored. First produce an annotated sketch for some sample data, then draw the logical data structure of the file in respect of the above problem.

Remember that the structure diagram should reflect the way that the data are to be processed, but it does not contain any processing detail such as 'accumulate the amounts' or 'display record'.

3.3.4 A payroll file has records for individual employees containing a department code.

    (a) A program is required to extract one specific department's data. Produce an annotated sketch of the payroll file, then draw a logical data structure.

    (b) If the file is sorted into ascending order of department code, draw a revised annotated sketch and logical data structure.

This exercise illustrates that, even though the problem is the same, different physical organisations of the same data will give rise to different logical structures.

3.3.5 Consider a customer file sorted by credit limit code within region code. The region code may have a value of A, B or C only. With the aid of an annotated sketch, draw the logical data structure for each of the following.

    (a) A program to count the number of records.

    (b) A program to count the number of records in region A.

    (c) A program to count the number of records in region C.

    (d) A program to sum the amount due of all records with credit limit code = 1.

    (e) A program to print the names of customers who have a credit limit of 4 who are not in region A.

This exercise illustrates that different problems give rise to different logical data structures for the same physical organisation.

3.3.6 A criminal record file is purged (that is, the redundant records are removed) according to the following criteria:

    (i) When the prisoner is released for offences carrying a sentence of less than two years.

    (ii) Three years after the prisoner is released for offences carrying a sentence of two years or more, unless the offence is murder when the record is not removed at all.

You may assume that murder will always carry a sentence of at least two years.

    Draw an annotated sketch and then a logical data structure in respect of the 'purging' program for each of the following:

    (a) The file is organised in ascending sequence of prison sentence term.

    (b) The file is organised into offence order (that is, all the burglaries together, all the murders together etc).

(c) The file is organised in alphabetic order of surname.

For this exercise, when drawing the sketch, it will be necessary to make a note of a number of nested selections after determining the possible effect of the physical organisation of the file.

3.3.7   A program is required to print each detail record of a transaction file together with an indication of the record type. In the file there may be three types of batch - credits, debits and account descriptions. Each batch has a batch header followed by any number of detail records. There may be any number of batches and they can occur in any order.

(a) Draw the annotated sketch and the logical data structure for the transaction file.

(b) Amend the above data structure to show that credit batches may contain 'cash' records and 'cheque' records in any order.

(c) Further amend the data structure to show that debit batches contain pairs of records - a sales record followed by a discount record.

3.3.8   A sales file contains a header record followed by details for several salesmen. For each salesman there will be a header record followed by sales detail records which are either 'cash' or 'account'.

(a) Draw an annotated sketch and the logical data structure for the sales file in respect of a program which is to display the 'cash' detail records and sum the amounts from the 'account' detail records for each salesman.

(b) Amend the above data structure to show an optional total record at the end of each group of salesman's records.

(c) Further amend the data structure to show that all 'cash' sales values of £10 or more attract a discount which has to be highlighted in the output.

4 Program Structures

4.1 Identifying correspondences

A correct program structure will 'mirror' the data structures of its input and output. So we now consider how to produce a program structure by combining the logical data structures (at this stage we will assume a maximum of one input and one output structure).

This means starting at the highest level and looking for components of the data structures which correspond in the sense that the whole of one component is used (or processed) to produce the whole of the other.

Particularly, the components should correspond in that the data represented by the corresponding components of the data structures must occur in the same order, and there should be the same number of each. Consider the structures shown in figure 4.1.

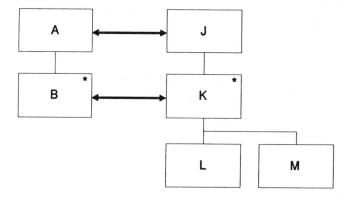

Figure 4.1

Starting from the top, A corresponds with J because there is one of each and we process A to obtain J. B corresponds with K if we process B to obtain K and the data which they represent can be shown diagrammatically as in figure 4.2.

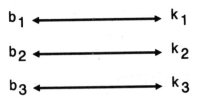

Figure 4.2

Note that the data satisfies the rules:
       1. Same order.
       2. Same number of each.
       3. Output derived from input.

Components B and K would not correspond in the cases shown in figure 4.3.

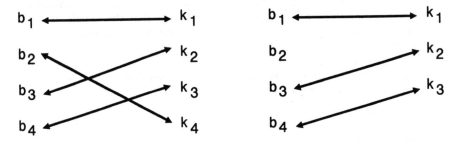

Figure 4.3

Having identified correspondences we indicate them by drawing a line between the corresponding components as in figure 4.1. If we are to produce the program structure from the data structures, we must ensure that each component corresponds with no more than one component from another data structure.

4.2 Combining data structures to produce program structures

We shall illustrate the approach by considering examples.

Example 1

We have a serial file of records and we wish to print them one record per line. The input file data structure is simply an iteration of records for printing and the output file data structure is an iteration of lines (each

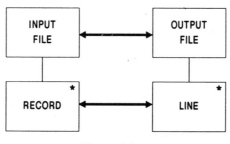

Figure 4.4

containing one record), as shown in figure 4.4.

Combining these data structures is easy because INPUT FILE corresponds with OUTPUT FILE and RECORD corresponds with LINE.

How so? In the first case, there is one input file that will be processed to produce one output file. In the second case, one record is processed to produce one line; and record and line are in the same order (record *n* of the input file will be printed on line *n*).

The components that correspond can now be combined to give the program structure exactly common to both of the data structures; see figure 4.5.

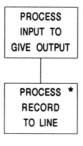

Figure 4.5

Example 2

Extending the above example, suppose we wanted to print a report heading at the start and a line containing a record count at the end. The data structures are as shown in figure 4.6.

The input file remains the same and the correspondences are the same as in the first example (INPUT FILE to REPORT FILE and RECORD to LINE).

The components REPORT HEADING, REPORT FILE BODY and RECORD COUNT, although appearing in only one of the data structures, do not cause any conflict. REPORT FILE BODY, in a sense, is necessary only because of the need to distinguish between the report heading, the body of the report and the record count.

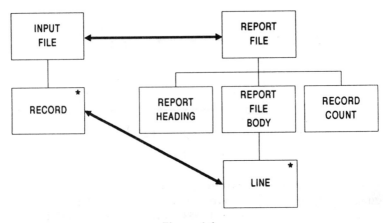

Figure 4.6

Then by combining these data structures at their points of correspondence we produce the program structure shown in figure 4.7.

In this case the relative positions of the components without correspondences are easily determined from the output structure. Note that the program structure also retains the logic of the input structure, in that PROCESS INPUT TO GIVE REPORT can be regarded indirectly (through the intermediate component PROCESS REPORT FILE BODY) as an iteration of PROCESS RECORD TO LINE.

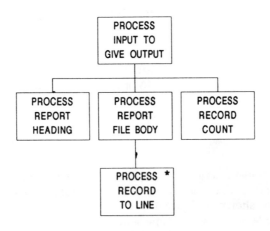

Figure 4.7

Example 3

Let us now consider an example that will be developed in later chapters.

We have a sales file which is sorted into year within sales area code. It is required to produce a report to show the sales details, with appropriate highlighting for low, medium and high sales (that is, a single exclamation mark when the sales value is less than 100, two exclamation marks when the sales value is between 100 and 300, and three exclamation marks for greater than 300). Headings are required for each area and totals are to be produced at relevant control breaks, that is, at change of year and area code.

To help us visualise the relevant order and groupings of both the input sales file and the output report, we produce annotated sketches emphasising the logic of the problem. These sketches are shown as figures 4.8 and 4.9. The data structures indicating correspondences are shown in figure 4.10.

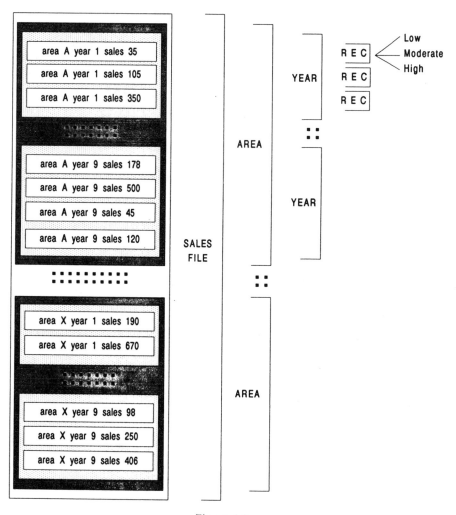

Figure 4.8

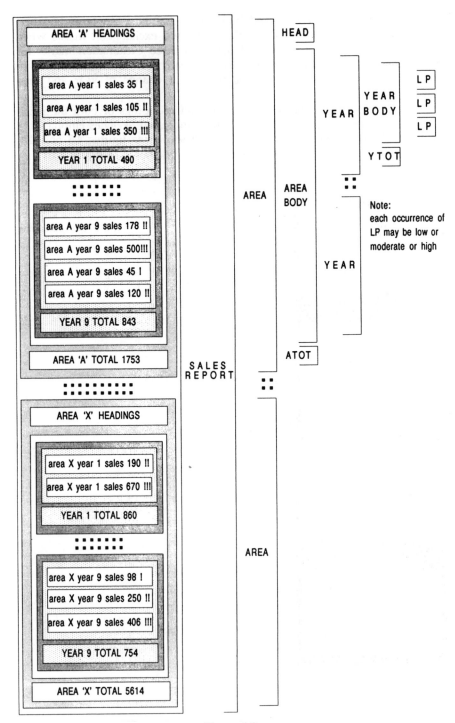

Figure 4.9

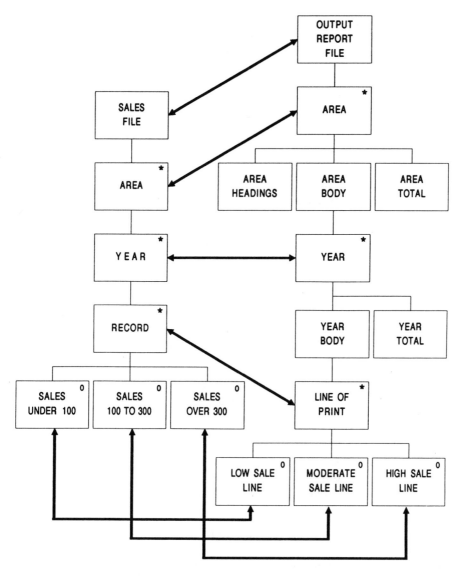

Figure 4.10

In respect of the problem under consideration, for each record in the input file there are three possibilities that are relevant: sales under 100, sales between 100 and 300, and sales over 300. There are also three different lines of print, depending on whether the sales are low, moderate or high. Thus both data structures contain a selection at the lowest level.

Once again, using the criteria of 'processing the whole of one component to produce the other, and order and number of data', identifying the

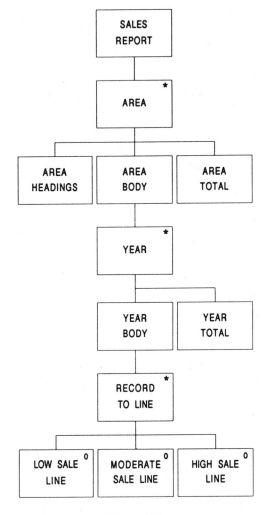

Figure 4.11

correspondences is straightforward. Fortunately, both files are sorted by year within area code and each detail line of print is obtained by processing the corresponding sales record. The positions of the non-corresponding components in the program structure are given by the output structure - see figure 4.11.

Since it can be taken as read, we shall not include 'PROCESS' in naming program structure components from now on.

The program structure (figure 4.11) again retains the logic of both data structures. You should be able to perceive the SALES FILE structure through intermediate components.

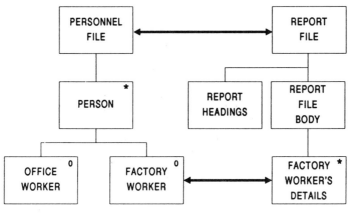

Figure 4.12

Example 4

A personnel file contains records of factory and office workers. A report, with headings, giving details of the factory workers is required. The data structures are given in figure 4.12.

A comparison with the previous example raises two questions.

Why have we not included the selection parts on the REPORT FILE? Simply because there are no office workers' details on the output file. The selection parts are on the PERSONNEL FILE because that is where the data that enables us to distinguish between an office worker and a factory worker resides.

Why does FACTORY WORKER'S DETAILS correspond with FACTORY WORKER? Simply because the correspondence satisfies our criteria; FACTORY WORKER'S DETAILS does not correspond with PERSON since, in general, there will be fewer FACTORY WORKER'S DETAIL lines than PERSON records.

It is also a little more difficult to produce the program structure. The position of PERSON relative to REPORT HEADINGS and REPORT FILE BODY is not obvious from the data structures, and the component part indicators of corresponding components do not match.

We overcome these problems by always merging the data structures such that:

1. Corresponding components are combined.
2. The logic of the data structures, as defined by the problem specification, is retained in the program structure.

PERSON cannot be a sequence of REPORT HEADINGS and REPORT FILE BODY, as this would include headings for each person and contradict the structure of REPORT FILE. However, making REPORT FILE BODY an

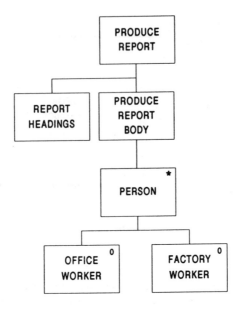

Figure 4.13

iteration of PERSON retains the required logic. The specification also requires us to retain the two selection parts, hence FACTORY WORKER'S DETAILS is combined with FACTORY WORKER as a selection part of PERSON. The program structure is shown in figure 4.13.

Again, you should be able to perceive the data structures in the program structure. So far as the output file is concerned, REPORT FILE BODY remains an iteration of FACTORY WORKER'S DETAILS because FACTORY WORKER is part of the iteration part PERSON.

It should be stressed that the program structure must always be derived from the data structures. As mentioned in chapter 1, one of the requirements of a software design method is that errors should be identified as soon as possible. Logical data structures that are difficult to combine may well, though not necessarily, contain errors. If you have any difficulty combining data structures or cannot find correspondences, first check that the logical data structures are correct in respect of the problem to be solved. The temptation to omit or introduce components arbitrarily should be resisted in favour of re-examining the data structures.

Unfortunately there are times when the data structures are correct but it is still not possible to produce a correct program structure. This occurs when data structures contradict or clash with each other. Even this situation can be resolved as we shall see in chapter 9.

Now for some more exercises. Data structures are to be produced followed by program structures based entirely on the data structures.

4.3 Exercises

For each of the following six problem descriptions, follow the procedure as outlined below.

1. Sketch sample data for both input and output files and annotate the sketches to indicate groupings, repetitions and selections. As we require logical data structures, remember the hints given in chapter 3. For input, consider how you might solve the problem in terms of a box-file of cards. For output, the logical data structure represents what appears physically in the file.
2. Produce logical data structures for both input and output files.
3. Indicate correspondences between components of the data structures.
4. Derive a program structure entirely from the logical data structures. Do not be tempted to invent new components or omit any components at this stage.

4.3.1 A production file contains a number of records about machines, indicating whether or not they are due for replacement. It is required to produce a duplicate file with one extra record at the end containing a count of the machines which are due for replacement.

4.3.2 A hospital file contains records of staff and patients sorted into ascending order of surname within ward. It is required to print all the names of the staff in ward order, with a heading at the start of each ward.

4.3.3 A personnel file is sorted by grade of staff and contains records of employees' qualifications. It is required to produce a list of the number of staff in each grade who possess a degree. The record layout for the personnel file is as follows:

character positions 1 - 3 Grade of staff

4 - 20 Name

21   No. of 'O' levels

22   No. of 'A' levels

23   Degree (Y or N)

The output required is of the form:

XYZ COMPANY - EMPLOYEES WITH DEGREES

GRADE	NUMBER
1	23
6	15
12	16
15	0
100	10
TOTAL	64

Hints.

Not all of the detail contained in the input record is pertinent to the problem at hand. Remember that you are drawing logical data structures that describe the data in respect of this particular problem.

Your sketch of sample data may help to identify correspondences. It should be apparent that certain groups of records in the input file correspond to certain lines on the output.

4.3.4 A product file contains a number of product records. Each record contains an area code, a district code, a product code and a value. The file is sorted into product within district within area. A program is required to select certain product codes and produce a report showing district and area totals of the values of the selected products in the order implied by the product file.

4.3.5 A student application file contains records which hold the status of applicants. The file is sorted into ascending order of course code. For each course there may be records of applicants who have merely been offered a place, followed by records of applicants who have been offered a place and 'accepted it, followed by records of applicants who have been rejected.

(a) It is required to print a listing, containing a report for each course of all rejected applicants in ascending order of course code. The reports contain a heading followed by the various applicants' names (one per line) followed by a total of such names. Note that the logic of the problem means that we need not differentiate between the batches of applicants who have been offered places and the batches of applicants who have accepted places.

(b) It is further required to produce a file containing records of accepted applicants in ascending order of course code. This is the first problem you have encountered with more than one output. You will need to draw correspondences between each output file and the input file, before combining all three to produce the program structure.

4.3.6 A payroll file is sorted by employee number and contains records of employees' pay details. Included in each employee record is a group of ten deductions which are specified by a code followed by an amount. It is required to produce a report showing those employees who pay deduction code 20. The format of the output is:

EMPLOYEES PAYING UNION FEES

NAME	AMOUNT
B. JONES	1.10
F. SMITH	3.50
R. BROWN	2.75
TOTAL	7.35

There is at most one occurrence of deduction code 20 in a record. If that deduction code is present, it can be in any of the ten elements of the deduction group.

Ideally we should stop examining the deduction group once the required deduction has been found. However, to avoid using an advanced technique explained in chapter 10, you may assume an examination of all elements of the group.

5 Elementary Program Operations and Conditions

5.1 Listing the conditions

When we are happy with our program structure, we are then in a position to think about the elementary program operations that must be included within the structure, and the conditions that control the iterations and selections. First we identify and list the conditions.

For each iteration we require a terminating condition, so we ask:

'How will the end of the iteration be detected?'
or:
'What condition must always be true for the iteration to continue?'.

Note that the answer to the first question gives the terminating condition directly, but the answer to the second gives the condition for the iteration to continue, which must therefore be negated.

Using the 'sales report' program structure from chapter 4 (see figure 5.1), let us list the conditions for the iterations.

The iteration SALES REPORT is concluded when there are no more AREAs to process. Or put another way, the iteration continues while there are AREAs to process. In other words the condition is

process SALES REPORT until end of sales file.

Note that, at this stage, the conditions are written in a form that is independent of any programming language (that is, end of sales file).

The definition of an iteration (see chapter 2) allows for SALES REPORT to be an iteration of zero AREAs (that is, the loop may not be entered). To allow for this we must assume that the condition is tested at the start of the loop. While there is a case to be made for an iteration construct of at least one occurrence, as well as the one we have already defined, we shall not draw this distinction.

The iteration AREA BODY continues while there are YEARs of the current AREA to process. How can we detect that there are no more YEARs

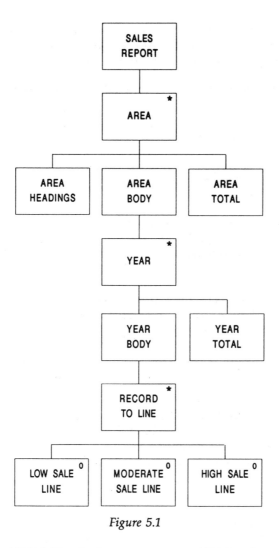

Figure 5.1

of the current AREA? Clearly there are no more YEARs of any AREA at the end of the file, so that must come into it. Further, when a new AREA is to be processed, there are no more YEARs for the old AREA. The condition then is a compound one:

process AREA BODY until end of sales file or a change of area.

In this nested loop situation, the condition for the outer loop (in this case 'end of sales file') should always be included as part of the condition for the inner loop. This ensures that the inner loop will eventually terminate even though 'a change of area' may not be detected.

One can use similar reasoning to determine the condition for the iteration YEAR BODY. One recognises the end of the records that relate to a particular YEAR for a particular AREA when the YEAR changes, or when the AREA changes, or when the end of the file is reached. So:

process YEAR BODY until end of sales file or a change of area or a change of year.

For the selections, we ask:

'What must be true for each of the options?'
'Are the conditions mutually exclusive?'
'Is the last option covered by ELSE?'

For the selection RECORD TO LINE, we need two conditions. There are three choices, but we have made the decision that the last selection part shall always be conditionless (that is, will be reached by ELSE). The conditions are:

select LOW SALE LINE if sales value < 100
else select MODERATE SALE LINE if sales value <= 300
else select HIGH SALE LINE.

This gives a condition list as follows:

C1   Until end of sales file
C2   Until end of sales file or change of area
C3   Until end of sales file or change of area or change of year
C4   If sales value < 100
C5   If sales value <= 300 (and >= 100)

5.2 Listing the elementary program operations

The elementary program operations can be listed by studying the program specification and taking cognisance of the program structure and conditions. What do we mean by elementary program operations? Here we will not consider the operations in terms of any particular programming language, but rather, entities that we know will be very easily converted to one or more program language statements.

We can tackle this part of the design in steps.

1. List the program initialisation and finalisation operations such as open and close files.
2. Identify the input records or components and hence list the input operations.

3. Identify the output records or components and hence list the output operations.
4. Identify any computations or transformations from input to output necessary to produce the detailed aspects of the required results.
5. List any detailed initialisation operations that will be required.
6. List any operations necessary to support the condition list.

In our 'sales report' program, the program initialisation and finalisation operations are:

1	Open files
2	Close files
3	Stop

There is only one input operation:

4	Read a sales file record

The principal operations to produce the required output are:

5	Print area headings
6	Print area total
7	Print year total
8	Print a low sales line
9	Print a moderate sales line
10	Print a high sales line

Operations 6 and 7 require some computation, hence:

11	Add to area total
12	Add to year total

The above, in turn, require initialisation operations:

13	Initialise area total to zero
14	Initialise year total to zero

Finally two operations are necessary because we need to be able to compare the AREA (or YEAR) of the record just read with the AREA (or YEAR) currently being processed. This is in order to construct the conditions 'change of year' and 'change of area' for the iterations YEAR BODY and AREA BODY.

15	Store area code
16	Store year

5.3 Allocating the conditions and operations

Allocation of the conditions is simple. We simply draw up a condition list and then write the appropriate reference above and to the right of the iteration or selection component part, as illustrated by the 'sales report' program structure (figure 5.2).

Allocation of the program operations takes more thought, but should not present any difficulties. If we have difficulty deciding where a particular operation is to be performed in respect of a program structure, there are three possible causes:

1. We do not need the operation, in that case we should re-examine the problem specification.
2. The program structure is deficient, in that case we must go back to the data structures.
3. The operation implies a condition, in that case we need to be more specific in our choice of operations.

Figure 5.2 shows the 'sales report' program structure with the operation numbers added to it in appropriate places. We shall now discuss how the decisions for allocation were arrived at. Basically, for each operation we ask two questions:

1. How many times and where in the program structure should the operation be executed? This identifies the component.
2. Should it be executed at the beginning, the middle or the end of the identified component?

All operations are allocated to elementary components. In some cases the component already exists (for example, 6 is allocated to AREA TOTAL); in other cases we effectively create a component (for example, the allocation of 2 and 3). When allocating an operation to a component already containing operations, you should ascertain its correct position relative to those already allocated (see operation 3 below).

Let us ask the above questions of the operations. We will leave operation number 4 for the moment.

Operation 1 (open files)
　　Once per program execution (SALES REPORT)
　　At the beginning.
Operation 2 (close files)
　　Once per program execution (SALES REPORT)
　　At the end.
Operation 3 (stop)
　　Once per program execution (SALES REPORT)
　　At the end (after operation 2).

Operation 5 (print area headings)
   Once per area (AREA)
   At the beginning (AREA HEADINGS).
Operation 6 (print area total)
   Once per area (AREA)
   At the end (AREA TOTAL).
Operation 7 (print year total)
   Once per year (YEAR)
   At the end (YEAR TOTAL).
Operation 8 (print a low sales line)
   Once per record with sales under 100 (LOW SALE LINE)
   Not applicable.
Operation 9 (print a moderate sales line)
   Once per record with 100 <= sales <= 300 (MODERATE SALE LINE)
   Not applicable.
Operation 10 (print a high sales line)
   Once per record with sales > 300 (HIGH SALE LINE)
   Not applicable.
Operation 11 (add to area total)
   Once per record (RECORD TO LINE)
   Beginning or end.
Operation 12 (add to year total)
   Once per record (RECORD TO LINE)
   Beginning or end.
Operation 13 (initialise area total to zero)
   Once per area (AREA)
   At the beginning (AREA HEADINGS).
Operation 14 (initialise year total to zero)
   Once per year (YEAR)
   At the beginning.
Operation 15 (store area code)
   Once per area (AREA)
   At the beginning (AREA HEADINGS).
Operation 16 (store year)
   Once per year (YEAR)
   At the beginning.

For operation 4 (read a sales file record) we apply a rule:

> We should read immediately after opening the file and again as soon
> as a record has been processed.

So we allocate operation 4 immediately after operation 1 and at the end
of RECORD TO LINE after operations 11 and 12.

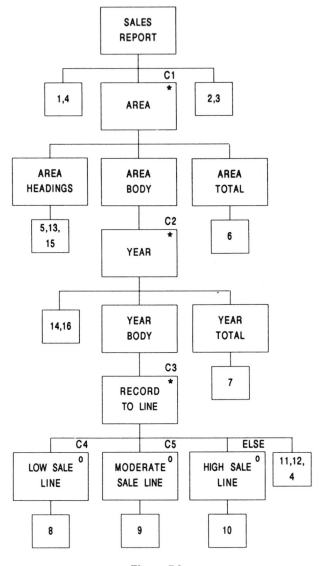

Figure 5.2

This completes the allocation, but the creation of extra elementary component boxes has disturbed the rules of construction:

> SALES REPORT now appears to be both a sequence and an iteration, RECORD TO LINE appears to be both a sequence and a selection.

To overcome this, we insert 'BODY' boxes at appropriate points; see figure 5.3.

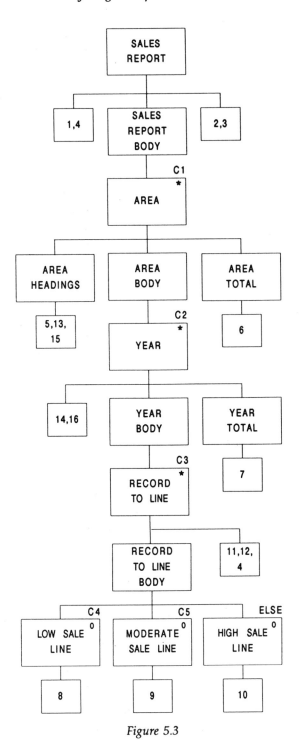

Figure 5.3

Once we have produced a revised program structure with allocated operations and conditions, we can check the design before proceeding to later stages of program production. A systematic method of doing this (by means of a trace table) is shown in section 13.1.2 of chapter 13.

5.4 Exercises

5.4.1 to 5.4.6

For each of the exercises at the end of chapter 4, except 4.3.5(a):

(a) List the operations and conditions.
(b) Allocate the conditions.
(c) Allocate the operations (after applying the two questions discussed in this chapter).
(d) Make any necessary revisions to the program structure by inserting appropriate 'BODY' boxes.

You will need to refer back to the exercises at the end of chapter 4 and then use the program structures given as the answers to those exercises.

6 Schematic Logic

6.1 Production of schematic logic (pseudo-code)

Schematic logic is a pseudo-code representation of the program structure with allocated operations and conditions. We will first produce schematic logic, then code the program in a high level programming language. Most programmers find it easier to translate the pseudo-code, rather than the program structure diagram, into the target language. Furthermore, when using one of the more advanced JSP techniques (covered in chapter 10), we shall find it necessary to amend the schematic logic, by introducing additional operations and conditions, without changing the program structure.

Let us describe the production of schematic logic for each of the three basic constructs, then put it all together for a whole program.

(a) Sequence - see figure 6.1

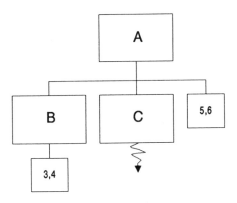

Figure 6.1

Here, A is a sequence of B (which has two operations, 3 then 4) followed by C (of unknown construct type) followed by the operations 5 then 6.

The schematic logic for this is given as figure 6.2. Notice that we specify

```
A SEQ              [construct-name - type
  B
    DO 3,4
  B END
  C ....           [component C is not defined but
    ....           it has a start and an end and
  C END            comes after B]
    DO 5,6
A END
```

Figure 6.2

the construct name followed by the type of construct.

Elementary components are shown as construct name without type (for example, B). Elementary operations are shown as DO statements either with or without operation descriptions. For example

```
        DO 1,4
or
        DO 1 [open files
        DO 4 [read a sales file record
```

(b) Iteration - see figure 6.3

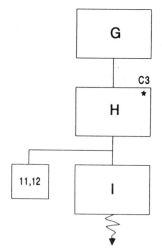

Figure 6.3

Here, G is an iteration of H, which is a sequence of the elementary component with operations 11 and 12, followed by the component I. Remember that it is component G that is the iteration construct, not H which is the component part of the iteration.

```
G ITER UNTIL C3 [construct-name - type - condition
  H SEQ
    DO 11,12
    I ....
      ....
    I END
  H END
G END
```

Figure 6.4

The schematic logic for this example is given as figure 6.4. Notice here that the condition that controls the iteration (C3) is written after the component name G, the type ITER and the word UNTIL.

c) *Selection - see figure 6.5*

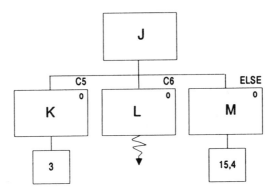

Figure 6.5

Here, J is a selection of K (which has the operation 3), or L (of unknown construct type), or M (which has the operations 15 then 4). Recall that with a selection, the last component part has no specified condition; it is controlled by the 'else' situation (that is, when the other conditions are all false).

The schematic logic is shown as figure 6.6. Here we see the condition IF C5 given after the component name J and type SEL. Also, the first alternative is specified by repeating the component name followed by the word ELSE 1 and the condition IF C6. The last (second) alternative does not have a condition, hence it is written as component name J followed by ELSE 2 only.

In the three examples above you will notice how the indentation matches the program structure. The convention used here, and in the following examples, is to indent by two spaces in the schematic logic for each level of the structure. You may decide to emphasise the levels of structure by using deeper indentation.

```
J SEL IF C5        [construct-name - type - condition
  K
     DO 3
  K END
J ELSE 1 IF C6    [name - 1st alternative - condition
  L ....
     ....
  L END
J ELSE 2          [name - 2nd (last) alternative - no condition
  M
     DO 15,4
  M END
J END
```

Figure 6.6

(d) *An example of all three combined - see figure 6.7*

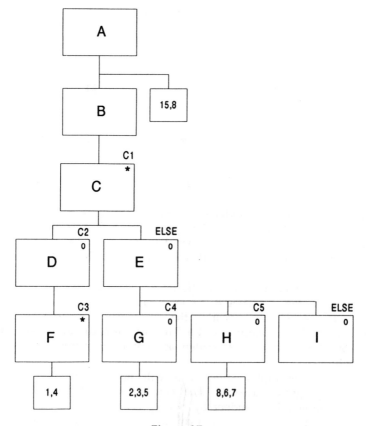

Figure 6.7

```
A SEQ
  B ITER UNTIL C1
    C SEL IF C2
      D ITER UNTIL C3
        F
            DO 1,4
        F END
      D END
    C ELSE 1
      E SEL IF C4
        G
            DO 2,3,5
        G END
      E ELSE 1 IF C5
        H
            DO 8,6,7
        H END
      E ELSE 2
        I
            [note - no operations
        I END
      E END
    C END
  B END
  DO 15,8
A END
```

Figure 6.8

Sometimes, as illustrated by I in figure 6.7, a component part of a selection has no elementary operations. In this case we still include the construct in our schematic logic (possibly with a comment to emphasise the 'passive' component).

The schematic logic is shown in figure 6.8.

6.2 Schematic logic for a complete program

Can we now tackle the production of schematic logic for the program structure for the 'sales report' program? You will find the program structure with allocated operations and conditions in figure 5.3. The schematic logic is shown in figure 6.9.

Check that figure 6.9 is an accurate translation of the program structure (figure 5.3) in chapter 5. Notice how the indentation of the schematic logic matches the number of levels in the program structure.

```
SALES REPORT SEQ
  DO 1 [open files
  DO 4 [read a sales file record
  SALES REPORT BODY ITER UNTIL C1 [end of sales file
    AREA SEQ
      AREA HEADINGS
        DO 5  [print area headings
        DO 13 [initialise area total to zero
        DO 15 [store area code
      AREA HEADINGS END
      AREA BODY ITER UNTIL C2 [end of sales file
                                  or change of area
        YEAR SEQ
          DO 14 [initialise year total to zero
          DO 16 [store year
          YEAR BODY ITER UNTIL C3 [end of sales file or change
                                      of area or change of year
            RECORD TO LINE SEQ
              RECORD TO LINE BODY SEL IF C4 [if sales < 100
                LOW SALE LINE
                  DO 8 [print a low sales line
                LOW SALE LINE END
              RECORD TO LINE BODY ELSE 1 IF C5 [if sales <= 300
                                                  (and >= 100)
                MODERATE SALE LINE
                  DO 9 [print a moderate sales line
                MODERATE SALE LINE END
              RECORD TO LINE BODY ELSE 2
                HIGH SALE LINE
                  DO 10 [print a high sales line
                HIGH SALE LINE END
              RECORD TO LINE BODY END
              DO 11 [add to area total
              DO 12 [add to year total
              DO 4  [read a sales file record
            RECORD TO LINE END
          YEAR BODY END
          YEAR TOTAL
            DO 7 [print year total
          YEAR TOTAL END
        YEAR END
      AREA BODY END
      AREA TOTAL
        DO 6 [print area total
      AREA TOTAL END
    AREA END
  SALES REPORT BODY END
  DO 2 [close files
  DO 3 [stop
SALES REPORT END
```

Figure 6.9

6.3 Exercises

6.3.1 to 6.3.6

The exercises at the end of chapter 5 asked you to produce program structures with allocated operations and conditions. For each of these, produce the schematic logic. You will note that the solutions include descriptions for each condition and elementary operation, as in figure 6.9; you may omit these descriptions.

If you wish, you may now attempt the case study in appendix B.

7 Implementation in a High Level Programming Language

7.1 From schematic logic to target language

The production of schematic logic, an elementary program operation list and condition list, essentially concludes the design stage. It remains only to translate these into a high level programming language. This involves:

1. Coding the declaration part of the program (as required by COBOL and Pascal for example).
2. Implementing the schematic constructs - SEQ, SEL and ITER - using control constructs provided by the target language.
3. Translating each elementary operation and condition into the target language, bearing in mind that certain operations will require more than one program statement.

We shall illustrate this coding process for Pascal and COBOL. For each language we provide rules for implementation of the three basic constructs using the schematic logic examples from the previous chapter with 'OPE-RATION N' and 'CONDITION CN' denoting the appropriate coding for 'Do N' and 'CN'; then we illustrate the complete process by producing a working program for the 'sales report' problem.

Though the reader may adopt different conventions regarding indentation, the use of lower and upper case and the amount of schematic logic retained in the program as comments, it is suggested that the control logic of the rules given in the following sections should be adhered to. The experienced programmer will observe that there are obvious alternatives to the coding rules; we have used rules in this chapter that retain the structure of the schematic logic.

As can be seen from the following sections, converting the schematic logic constructs into a target language is a 'mechanical' process based on simple rules. Software packages that perform this process are now widely available. Typically, a JSP pre-processor requires input in the form of a declaration section, elementary operation list and condition list, all in the target language, followed by the schematic logic. The resulting output is a complete, coded program.

7.2 Pascal as target language

The block structure of Pascal is identical to that used in the schematic logic; their control constructs are almost identical - the only difference being the operation of the controlling predicates in the ITER and WHILE constructs (see below). The Pascal code will therefore closely resemble the schematic logic.

(a) Sequence and elementary component

The sequence parts are retained in the same order as they appear in the schematic logic - see figure 7.1.

A SEQ	(* A seq *)

B
    DO 3,4
B END
	(* B *)
	    OPERATION 3
	    OPERATION 4
	(* B end *)

C .... C END	(* C ...... *) .... (* C END *)
DO 5,6	OPERATION 5 OPERATION 6
A END	(* A end *)

Figure 7.1

Hence the rules for coding a sequence or elementary component are:
1. At the start:
    create a comment, such as (* component name seq *) or (* component name *).
2. At the end:
    create a comment, such as (* component name end *).

(b) Iteration

Pascal provides both a 'WHILE condition DO statement(s)' construct and a 'REPEAT statement(s) UNTIL condition' construct. The condition in the REPEAT construct is tested at the end of the loop. The iteration will therefore always occur at least once. Since it does not allow for zero occurrences the REPEAT statement should not be used to code the ITER construct.

The WHILE statement, with the condition tested at the head of the loop, does allow for zero or more occurrences. However, for the ITER construct the iteration stops when the condition is true; for the WHILE statement the iteration stops when the condition is false. The ITER construct is therefore coded by means of the WHILE statement with the negation of the ITER condition - see figure 7.2.

G ITER UNTIL C3	(* G iter *)
	WHILE NOT (CONDITION C3) DO
	BEGIN
H SEQ	(* H seq *)
DO 11,12	OPERATION 11
I	OPERATION 12
....	(* I ...... *)
I END	....
H END	(* I END *)
	(* H end *)
	END ;
G END	(* G end *)

Figure 7.2

The coding rules for an iteration are:
  1. At the start:
       create a comment, such as (* component name iter *);
       use the WHILE construct with the negation of the ITER condition.
  2. At the end:
       create a comment, such as (* component name end *).

(c) Selection

The SEL ... ELSE ... construct translates directly into the Pascal 'IF condition THEN statement(s) ELSE statement(s)' construct - see figure 7.3.
  The coding rules for a selection are:
  1. At the start:
       create a comment, such as (* component name sel *);
       use the IF....THEN part of the IF....THEN....ELSE.... construct with the appropriate condition from the condition list.
  2. At ELSE n:
       create a comment, such as (* component name else n *);
       use the ELSE IF....THEN part of the IF....THEN....ELSE.... construct with the appropriate condition from the condition list, except for the last ELSE n where there is no condition.
  3. At the end:
       create a comment, such as (* component name end *).

J SEL IF C5	(* J sel *) IF CONDITION C5 THEN

K
  DO 3
K END
	(* K *)
	    OPERATION 3
	(* K end *)

J ELSE 1 IF C6	(* J else 1 *) ELSE IF CONDITION C6 THEN
L .... L END	BEGIN (* L .... *) .... (* L end *) END
J ELSE 2	(* J ELSE 2 *) ELSE

M
  DO 15,4
M END
	BEGIN
	(* M *)
	    OPERATION 15
	    OPERATION 4
	(* M end *)
	END ;

J END	(* J end *)

Figure 7.3

(d) Complete program

We shall now code a complete program (see figure 6.9 for the schematic logic of the 'sales report' example) using the following approach.

1. Inspect the problem specification and hence declare those variables required for input and output, such as **salesrec, salesfile** and **reportfile**.
2. Inspect the elementary operations and conditions and hence declare any additional data items that will be required, such as **storedyear**.
3. Code the executable part of the program from the schematic logic, using the above rules for the control constructs and translating operations and conditions into Pascal. For example

5   Print area headings

becomes

```
Writeln (reportfile,'AREA ',area) ;
Writeln (reportfile) ;
```

As each operation and condition is coded,

(i) check that appropriate variables have been declared;
(ii) to prevent recoding of an operation or condition already used and

to ensure that they are all eventually coded, tick each one off on the appropriate list.

As can be seen from the above example and the program shown in figure 7.4, an elementary operation may require more than one program statement.

Note that the solution in figure 7.4 asssumes that the last record on the input file is a dummy record (sentinel) with Z as the area code. End of file can then be detected by **area = 'Z'**.

```
PROGRAM Sales (salesfile, reportfile) ;

TYPE
    recordtype      = RECORD
                          area            : char ;
                          year            : 0..99 ;
                          salesproduct    : PACKED ARRAY [1..20]
                                                  OF char ;
                          salesamount     : 0..999 ;
                      END ;

VAR
    storedarea      : char ;
    storedyear      : 0..99 ;
    areatotal,
    yeartotal       : 0..99999 ;
    salesrec        : recordtype ;
    salesfile       : FILE OF recordtype ;
    reportfile      : text ;

BEGIN
(* sales report seq *)
  Reset (salesfile) ;
  Rewrite (reportfile) ;
  Read (salesfile, salesrec) ;
  WITH salesrec DO
  (* sales report body iter *)
  WHILE NOT (area = 'Z') DO
    BEGIN
    (* area seq *)
      (* area headings *)
        Writeln (reportfile, 'AREA  ', area) ;
        Writeln (reportfile) ;
        areatotal := 0 ;
        storedarea := area ;
      (* area headings end *)
      (* area body iter *)
      WHILE NOT ((area = 'Z') OR (storedarea <> area)) DO
        BEGIN
```

Figure 7.4 above and opposite

```
              (* year seq *)
                yeartotal := 0 ;
                storedyear := year ;
                (* year body iter *)
              WHILE NOT ((area = 'Z') OR (storedarea <> area) OR
                  (storedyear <> year)) DO
                  BEGIN
                  (* record to line seq *)
                    (* record to line body sel *)
                    IF salesamount < 100 THEN
                      (* low sale line *)
                        Writeln (reportfile, salesproduct:20,
                          salesamount:8, ' |')
                      (* low sale line end *)
                    (* record to line body else 1 *)
                    ELSE IF salesamount <= 300 THEN
                      (* moderate sale line *)
                        Writeln (reportfile, salesproduct:20,
                          salesamount:8, ' ||')
                      (* moderate sale line end *)
                    (* record to line body else 2 *)
                    ELSE
                      (* high sale line *)
                        Writeln (reportfile, salesproduct:20,
                          salesamount:8, ' |||') ;
                      (* high sale line end *)
                    (* record to line body end *)
                    areatotal := areatotal + salesamount ;
                    yeartotal := yeartotal + salesamount ;
                    Read (salesfile, salesrec) ;
                  (* record to line end *)
                   END ;
                (* year body end *)
                (* year total *)
                  Writeln (reportfile) ;
                  Writeln (reportfile, 'YEAR TOTAL ':23, yeartotal:5);
                  Writeln (reportfile) ;
                (* year total end *)
              (* year end *)
              END ;
          (* area body end *)
          (* area total *)
            Writeln (reportfile) ;
            Writeln (reportfile, 'AREA TOTAL ':23, areatotal:5) ;
            Writeln (reportfile) ;
            Writeln (reportfile) ;
          (* area total end *)
        (* area end *)
        END ;
    (* sales report body end *)
  (* sales report end *)
END.
```

7.3 COBOL as target language

The following examples illustrate how the schematic logic can be translated directly into COBOL code. We have not used the PERFORM verb in the coding rules because to do so would give a disjointed translation. A performed routine would not appear in the same relative position within the COBOL code as that of the corresponding pseudo-code within the schematic logic. Chapter 11 gives reasons why the use of PERFORM is not recommended when using the more advanced features of JSP, which are described in chapters 9 and 10.

(a) Sequence and elementary component

The sequence parts are retained in the same order as they appear in the schematic logic - see figure 7.5.

A SEQ	A-SEQ.
	B.
B	OPERATION 3
DO 3,4	OPERATION 4
B END	B-END.
C	C-......
....	....
C END	C-END.
	OPERATION 5
DO 5,6	OPERATION 6
A END	A-END.

Figure 7.5

The coding rules for a sequence or elementary component are:
  1. At the start:
       use the paragraph name COMPONENT-NAME-SEQ or
       COMPONENT-NAME.
  2. At the end:
       use the paragraph name COMPONENT-NAME-END.

(b) Iteration

We use the COBOL IF and GO TO statements to implement the ITER construct, as indicated in figure 7.6.

```
                                 G-ITER.
   G  ITER  UNTIL  C3                IF  CONDITION  C3
                                       GO  TO  G-END.

       H  SEQ           H-SEQ.
           DO  11,12        OPERATION  11
           I  ....          OPERATION  12
                         I-........
           ....
           I  END           ........
       H  END           I-END.
                         H-END.

                               GO  TO  G-ITER.
   G  END                G-END.
```

Figure 7.6

The coding rules for an iteration are:

  1. At the start:

      use the paragraph name COMPONENT-NAME-ITER;

      use an IF statement with the ITER condition and true action GO TO COMPONENT-NAME-END.

  2. At the end:

      use GO TO COMPONENT-NAME-ITER;

      use the paragraph name COMPONENT-NAME-END.

(c) Selection

Using the COBOL IF....THEN....ELSE and GO TO statements, as indicated in figure 7.7, enables us to retain the structure of the schematic logic.

  The coding rules for a selection are:

  1. At the start:

      use the paragraph name COMPONENT-NAME-SEL;

      use an IF statement with the SEL condition,

        true action NEXT SENTENCE,

        and false action GO TO COMPONENT-NAME-ELSE-1.

  2. At ELSE n:

      use GO TO COMPONENT-NAME-END;

      use the paragraph name COMPONENT-NAME-ELSE-N;

      then provided it is not the last ELSE, use an IF statement with the ELSE n condition,

        true action NEXT SENTENCE,

        and false action GO TO COMPONENT-NAME-ELSE-M (where M is N+1).

  3. At the end:

      use the paragraph name COMPONENT-NAME-END.

	J-SEL.
J SEL IF C5	IF CONDITION C5 NEXT SENTENCE ELSE GO TO J-ELSE-1

K
   DO 3
K END
	K.
	   OPERATION 3
	K-END.

J ELSE 1 IF C6	GO TO J-END. J-ELSE-1. IF CONDITION C6 NEXT SENTENCE ELSE GO TO J-ELSE-2.

L ....
  ....
L END
	L-.......
	  ....
	L-END.

J ELSE 2	GO TO J-END. J-ELSE-2.

M
   DO 15,4
M END
	M.
	   OPERATION 15
	   OPERATION 4
	M-END.

J END	J-END.

Figure 7.7

There is an alternative that could equally well be used. All the
    'IF condition
      NEXT SENTENCE
    ELSE
      GO TO next else' statements
could be replaced by
    'IF not condition
      GO TO next else'.

The slight disadvantage of having to negate the appropriate condition is balanced by not having to use the ELSE part of the IF statement.

(d) Complete program

We shall now code a complete program (see figure 6.9 for schematic logic of the 'sales report' example) using the following approach.

    1. Code the Identification Division, Environment Division and those parts of the Data Division required for input or output from the

problem specification. For example

```
01 AREA-HEADINGS.
   03 FILLER       PIC X(6) VALUE "AREA".
   03 AREA-HD      PIC X.
```

2. From an inspection of the elementary operations and conditions, include in the Data Division any additional data items that will be required such as STORED-YEAR.

3. Code the Procedure Division from the schematic logic, using the above rules for the control constructs and translating operations and conditions into COBOL. For example

5	Print area headings

becomes

```
MOVE IN-AREA TO AREA-HD
WRITE PRINT-LINE FROM AREA-HEADINGS
WRITE PRINT-LINE FROM SPACES AFTER 1.
```

As each operation or condition is coded:

(i) Check that appropriate data items have been included in the Data Division.

(ii) To prevent recoding of an operation or condition already used and to ensure that they are all coded, tick each one off on the appropriate list.

As can be seen from the above example and the program in figure 7.8, an elementary operation may require more than one program statement.

```
IDENTIFICATION DIVISION.
PROGRAM-ID. SALES.
ENVIRONMENT DIVISION.
INPUT-OUTPUT SECTION.
FILE-CONTROL.
    SELECT SALES-FILE ASSIGN TO "SALES.SEQ".
    SELECT OUTPUT-REPORT-FILE ASSIGN TO "SALES.LPT".
DATA DIVISION.
FILE SECTION.
FD   SALES-FILE.
01   SALES-REC.
     03 IN-AREA          PIC X.
     03 IN-YEAR          PIC 99.
     03 IN-PRODUCT       PIC X(20).
     03 IN-AMOUNT        PIC 999.
FD   OUTPUT-REPORT-FILE.
01   PRINT-LINE          PIC X(80).
WORKING-STORAGE SECTION.
01   AREA-HEADINGS.
     03 FILLER           PIC X(6)  VALUE "AREA".
     03 AREA-HD          PIC X.
01   YEAR-TOTAL-LINE.
     03 FILLER           PIC X(12) VALUE SPACES.
     03 FILLER           PIC X(11) VALUE "YEAR TOTAL".
     03 YEAR-TOT         PIC ZZZZ9.
01   AREA-TOTAL-LINE.
     03 FILLER           PIC X(12) VALUE SPACES.
     03 FILLER           PIC X(11) VALUE "AREA TOTAL".
     03 AREA-TOT         PIC ZZZZ9.
01   DETAIL-LINE.
     03 OUT-PRODUCT      PIC X(25).
     03 OUT-AMOUNT       PIC ZZ9.
     03 FILLER           PIC XX      VALUE SPACES.
     03 OUT-RATING       PIC X(3).
77   TOTAL-FOR-AREA      PIC 9(5).
77   TOTAL-FOR-YEAR      PIC 9(5).
77   STORED-AREA         PIC X.
77   STORED-YEAR         PIC 99.
PROCEDURE DIVISION.
SALES-REPORT-SEQ.
    OPEN INPUT SALES-FILE OUTPUT OUTPUT-REPORT-FILE.
    READ SALES-FILE AT END
        MOVE HIGH-VALUES TO SALES-REC.
SALES-REPORT-BODY-ITER.
    IF SALES-REC = HIGH-VALUES
        GO TO SALES-REPORT-BODY-END.
AREA-SEQ.
AREA-HEADINGS.
    MOVE IN-AREA TO AREA-HD
    WRITE PRINT-LINE FROM AREA-HEADINGS
    WRITE PRINT-LINE FROM SPACES AFTER 1.
    MOVE ZERO TO TOTAL-FOR-AREA.
    MOVE IN-AREA TO STORED-AREA.
AREA-HEADINGS-END.
AREA-BODY-ITER.
    IF SALES-REC = HIGH-VALUES OR IN-AREA NOT = STORED-AREA
        GO TO AREA-BODY-END.
YEAR-SEQ.
    MOVE ZERO TO TOTAL-FOR-YEAR.
```

Figure 7.8 above and opposite

```
        MOVE IN-YEAR TO STORED-YEAR.
YEAR-BODY-ITER.
        IF SALES-REC = HIGH-VALUES OR IN-AREA NOT = STORED-AREA
            OR IN-YEAR NOT = STORED-YEAR
            GO TO YEAR-BODY-END.
RECORD-TO-LINE-SEQ.
RECORD-TO-LINE-BODY-SEL.
        IF IN-AMOUNT < 100 NEXT SENTENCE
            ELSE GO TO RECORD-TO-LINE-BODY-ELSE-1.
LOW-SALE-LINE.
        MOVE IN-PRODUCT TO OUT-PRODUCT
        MOVE IN-AMOUNT TO OUT-AMOUNT
        MOVE "!" TO OUT-RATING
        WRITE PRINT-LINE FROM DETAIL-LINE AFTER 1.
LOW-SALE-LINE-END.
        GO TO RECORD-TO-LINE-BODY-END.
RECORD-TO-LINE-BODY-ELSE-1.
        IF IN-AMOUNT NOT > 300 NEXT SENTENCE
            ELSE GO TO RECORD-TO-LINE-BODY-ELSE-2.
MODERATE-SALE-LINE.
        MOVE IN-PRODUCT TO OUT-PRODUCT
        MOVE IN-AMOUNT TO OUT-AMOUNT
        MOVE "!!" TO OUT-RATING
        WRITE PRINT-LINE FROM DETAIL-LINE AFTER 1.
MODERATE-SALE-LINE-END.
        GO TO RECORD-TO-LINE-BODY-END.
RECORD-TO-LINE-BODY-ELSE-2.
HIGH-SALE-LINE.
        MOVE IN-PRODUCT TO OUT-PRODUCT
        MOVE IN-AMOUNT TO OUT-AMOUNT
        MOVE "!!!" TO OUT-RATING
        WRITE PRINT-LINE FROM DETAIL-LINE AFTER 1.
HIGH-SALE-LINE-END.
RECORD-TO-LINE-BODY-END.
        ADD IN-AMOUNT TO TOTAL-FOR-AREA.
        ADD IN-AMOUNT TO TOTAL-FOR-YEAR.
        READ SALES-FILE AT END
            MOVE HIGH-VALUES TO SALES-REC.
RECORD-TO-LINE-END.
        GO TO YEAR-BODY-ITER.
YEAR-BODY-END.
YEAR-TOTAL.
        MOVE TOTAL-FOR-YEAR TO YEAR-TOT
        WRITE PRINT-LINE FROM YEAR-TOTAL-LINE AFTER 2
        WRITE PRINT-LINE FROM SPACES AFTER 1.
YEAR-TOTAL-END.
YEAR-END.
        GO TO AREA-BODY-ITER.
AREA-BODY-END.
AREA-TOTAL.
        MOVE TOTAL-FOR-AREA TO AREA-TOT
        WRITE PRINT-LINE FROM AREA-TOTAL-LINE AFTER 2
        WRITE PRINT-LINE FROM SPACES AFTER 2.
AREA-TOTAL-END.
AREA-END.
        GO TO SALES-REPORT-BODY-ITER.
SALES-REPORT-BODY-END.
        CLOSE SALES-FILE OUTPUT-REPORT-FILE.
        STOP RUN.
SALES-REPORT-END.
```

7.4 Exercises

7.4.1　Code the program for exercise 4.3.1 in COBOL. The schematic logic is given in appendix A as solution 6.3.1. The record descriptions for the production files are given in figure 7.9.

```
01   PRODUCTION-RECORD.
     03 RECORD-TYPE          PIC 9.
        88 END-OF-FILE        VALUE 9.
     03 MACHINE              PIC X(20).
     03 DATE-PURCHASED       PIC X(8).
     03 REPLACEMENT          PIC 9.
        88 REPLACEMENT-DUE    VALUE 9.
01   COUNT-RECORD.
     03 FILLER              PIC 9
                            VALUE 8.
     03 REPLACE-COUNT       PIC 9(6).
```

Figure 7.9

7.4.2　Code the program for exercise 4.3.2 in Pascal. The schematic logic is given in appendix A as solution 6.3.2. The final record in the hospital file contains ZZZZ for ward as an end of file indicator. Use the type declarations shown in figure 7.10.

```
TYPE
   packed4      = PACKED ARRAY [1..4] OF char ;
   recordtype   = RECORD
                     ward    : packed4 ;
                     name    : PACKED ARRAY [1..20] OF char ;
                     patient : boolean ;
                  END ;
```

Figure 7.10

7.4.3　Code the program for exercise 4.3.3 In COBOL. The schematic logic is given in appendix A as solution 6.3.3. Use the personnel record description given in figure 7.11.

```
01   PERSONNEL-REC.
     03 GRADE         PIC 999.
     03 NAME          PIC X(17).
     03 O-LEVELS      PIC 9.
     03 A-LEVELS      PIC 9.
     03 DEGREE-Y-N    PIC X.
        88 HAS-DEGREE  VALUE "Y".
```

Figure 7.11

8 More Than One Input File

8.1 Merging data (at most, one record per key per file)

If we are to process more than one input file simultaneously, then very often the input files will have to be sorted into a specific order and, at the top level, will have very similar logical data structures.

One way of viewing such problems is that we must collate or merge the data from the input files in order to produce the required output. Such operations are done on the basis of matching key fields. Throughout this chapter, we assume that input files are sorted into ascending order of key value. At this stage we shall assume that there is, at most, one record per key per file.

The top level of the logical data structures for each input file in a collate or merge problem will inevitably indicate that the file is an iteration of each possible matching key - see figure 8.1.

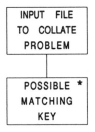

Figure 8.1

We use the term 'possible matching key' because each input file has the same set of allowable key values; so there is a potential for matching any key in one file with its corresponding key in another input file.

Furthermore, each possible key may or may not be present in a particular file, and is therefore a selection of either being present or absent. To illustrate this, consider two files containing records with unique keys - the range of possible key values being 1 to 4. The maximum number of possible records on each file is therefore 4. Let us say for file A that we have keys 1 and 3, and in file B that we have keys 2 and 3; that is

FILE A	FILE B
1	2
3	3

Clearly the presence or absence of a particular key value in a given file will have an effect on the collate process. Also the combinations of 'present' and 'absent' may indicate different processing actions (for example, if a record of a given key is present in file A only - copy the record to output; if present in both files - merge the data before output; if present in file B only - display an error message). The logical data structures for both files must therefore represent the following situation:

> key 1 is present or absent
> key 2 is present or absent
> key 3 is present or absent
> key 4 is present or absent

which gives the structure shown in figure 8.2.

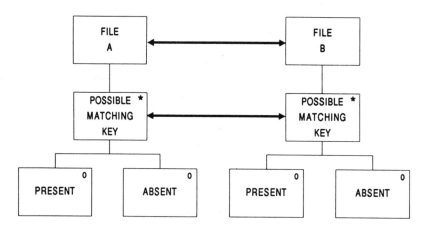

Figure 8.2

Notice that we did not regard FILE A as an iteration of KEY PRESENT ON A, nor FILE B as an iteration of KEY PRESENT ON B. Since these components do not correspond, we would not be able to combine the two input structures. So, how did we arrive at the above correspondences? The basic rule for more than one input file is that corresponding components must match. Clearly, FILE A and FILE B correspond. Since each file is an iteration of each possible key (1, 2, 3 and 4 in the above example), the components POSSIBLE MATCHING KEY also correspond. As for the selection parts, file A key present does not necessarily match with file B key present, and similarly for the other selection parts.

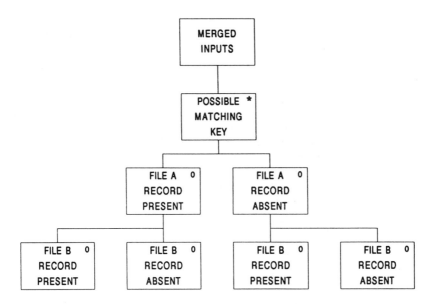

Figure 8.3

If we refer back to the simple key range of 1 to 4 only, there are obviously four combinations of 'PRESENT and ABSENT'. These combinations are obtained by combining both selection components from file B with each selection component in file A, as illustrated in the merged input structure, figure 8.3.

This can be simplified by regarding the selection POSSIBLE MATCHING KEY as having four component parts as shown in figure 8.4.

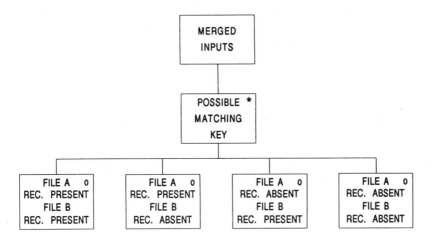

Figure 8.4

Further examination of the problem indicates that the fourth selection part, 'file A record absent and file B record absent', is only detectable if we process every possible key value (for example, by means of a key counter). If we are processing only those keys that actually occur in the input files, then this selection part does not appear on the combined input structure.

We can illustrate the difference in the two cases by solving the problem of counting the number of key values for each of the conditions. The output for such a problem is trivial, so our combined input structure becomes the program structure and we can proceed to allocate operations (which include the use of a key counter) to it. After we have solved this problem, we shall apply an operation list which does not include the use of a counter to a structure without the final selection part. The operation list including the use of a key counter is:

1	Open files
2	Close files
3	Stop
4	Read a file 'A' record
5	Read a file 'B' record
6	Print all totals
7	Add 1 to 'both present' total
8	Add 1 to 'A only' total
9	Add 1 to 'B only' total
10	Add 1 to 'both absent' total
11	Add 1 to key counter
12	Initialise all totals
13	Initialise key counter = 1

Allocating these to the program structure and including body boxes as required, gives the structure shown in figure 8.5 for the COLLATE PROBLEM WITH ALL POSSIBLE KEYS PROCESSED.

The condition list for this problem is:

C1	Until end of key range (key counter > maximum)
C2	If key counter = A key = B key
C3	If key counter = A key <> B key
C4	If key counter = B key <> A key

Note that the conditions C2, C3 and C4 will be affected by the way in which the target language handles end of file. For example, C3 in full should allow for the cases where end of file has been reached. That is

C3	If (key counter = A key and not end of file A) and (key counter <> B key or end of file B)

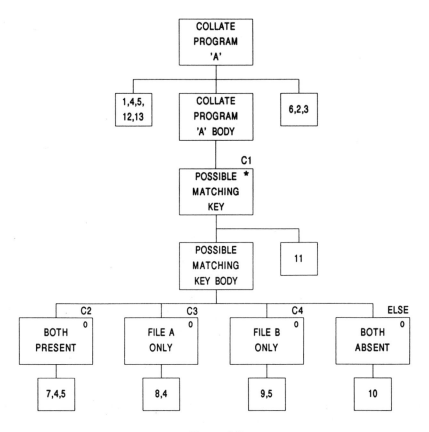

Figure 8.5

If, however, the key of each file is set to an impossibly high value when end of file is reached, then whenever end of file B is true, so is key counter <> B key; similarly, key counter = A key will ensure that we are not at the end of file A. Henceforth, we shall assume that end of file is handled in this way and use the above simplified versions of C2, C3 and C4.

Now let us turn our attention to the problem where we are interested in only the keys for which records are present in one or both input files. In this case, the data structures of figure 8.2 are combined to give a merged input structure which, assuming that only the appropriate totals are output, becomes the program structure - COLLATE PROBLEM WITH ONLY THOSE KEYS PRESENT ON ONE OR BOTH OF THE INPUT FILES PROCESSED - see figure 8.6.

For this problem we have a different condition list and, of course, do not need operations 10, 11 and 13 from the operation list.

C1	Until end of both files
C2	If A key = B key
C3	If A key < B key

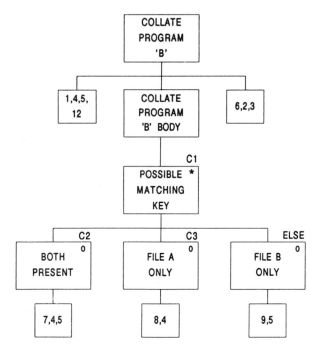

Figure 8.6

At this stage it should be stressed that, as file A and file B are both sequential files then, irrespective of the problem, we must retain the three selection component parts identified in figure 8.6. The reason is that we still need to process each record, even if this is merely reading past "unwanted records".

One further case, which follows from the above, occurs when we are required to process all records from one file only (file A) but selectively take into account any data that may be present for corresponding keys in another file (file B). In other words, we are interested in only two of the collate possibilities:

file A record present and file B record present;
file A record present and file B record absent.

In this case, we should make file B a direct access file. The 'read a file B record' operation (number 5 in our list) then becomes:

5   Attempt to read file B record with key = A key

Now, the data structures of figure 8.2 are combined to give a merged input structure which, assuming that only appropriate totals are output,

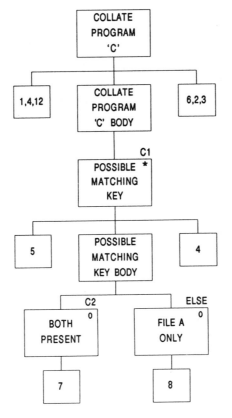

Figure 8.7

becomes the program structure - COLLATE PROBLEM WITH ONLY THOSE KEYS PRESENT ON ONE OF THE INPUT FILES PROCESSED - see figure 8.7.

Note that figure 8.7 needs only operations 1 to 8 and 12 (9, 10, 11 and 13 from the original list are obviously not required) and has only two conditions:

C1	Until end of file A
C2	If record found in direct access file B

In the above examples, we have virtually ignored the influence of output files so that we could concentrate on the merging of input files. Let us now consider a collate example with a simple output file.

In a payroll system, two sequential files are used: a wages file for weekly paid employees and a salaries file for monthly paid employees. Both files are sorted by employee number. An employee should not be present in both files, but it is thought that this might have occurred due to clerical errors. It is therefore required to produce a report with headings, the details of any employees who are on both files, and then totals of the number of records in each file.

Having drawn the data structures for both input files (see figure 8.2) and the output file, first we combine the input files and then draw correspondences between the output and the combined input, as shown in figure 8.8.

This gives us the program structure shown in figure 8.9.

The design would then be completed in the usual way by listing the operations and conditions and allocating them to the program structure.

It is recommended that exercises 8.4.1, 8.4.2 and 8.4.3 at the end of this chapter are attempted at this stage, before we go on to deal with more complex problems.

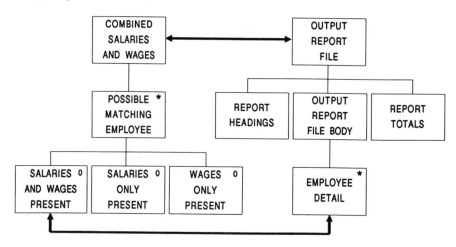

Figure 8.8

8.2 More complex merges (more than one record per key)

The solutions given above really only apply to the cases where there is, at most, one record per key per file. If we consider a problem where the two input files may have more than one record per key, we have extended data structures as shown in figure 8.10.

If we assume that all possible keys are processed and ignore the influence of an output data structure, the program structure derived from figure 8.10 is as detailed in figure 8.11.

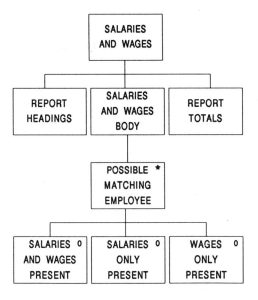

Figure 8.9

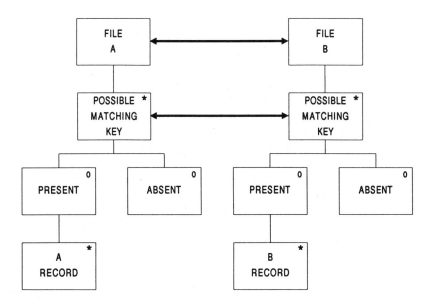

Figure 8.10

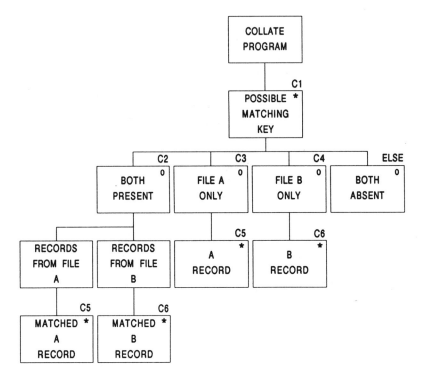

Figure 8.11

The condition list is as follows:

C1	Until end of key range
C2	If key counter = A key = B key
C3	If key counter = A key <> B key
C4	If key counter = B key <> A key
C5	Until end of A records of current key (A key <> key counter)
C6	Until end of B records of current key (B key <> key counter)

As in the previous section, we have simplified the structure by regarding POSSIBLE MATCHING KEY as a selection of four component parts.

BOTH PRESENT is shown as a sequence of RECORDS FROM FILE A followed by RECORDS FROM FILE B, because the iteration of A RECORD from the FILE A data structure and the iteration of B RECORD from the FILE B data structure must both occur as part of the component BOTH PRESENT.

Given the specific problem of counting all records that are matched, all that are in file A only, and all that are in file B only (that is, only those keys present on one or both of the files processed), the data structures of figure 8.10 are combined to give the program structure shown in figure 8.12.

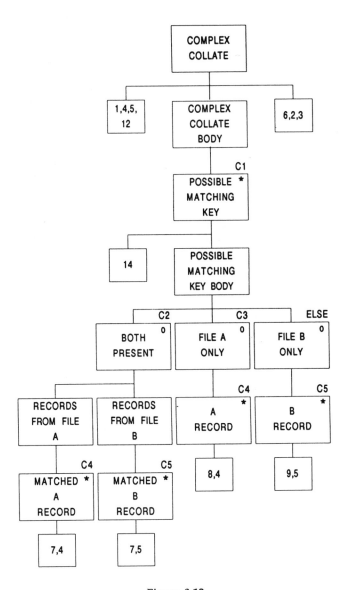

Figure 8.12

The condition list for this is:

C1	Until end of both input files
C2	If A key = B key
C3	If A key < B key
C4	Until change of key (A key <> stored key)
C5	Until change of key (B key <> stored key)

An additional operation to those used in the previous section is necessary in order to implement C4 and C5:

14	Store key (the lower of A and B)

8.3 The sequential file update

We can apply the collate problem solution to the sequential file update problem. Assuming, at most, one record per key per file, the data structures of an input and output master file and a transaction file are as shown in figure 8.13.

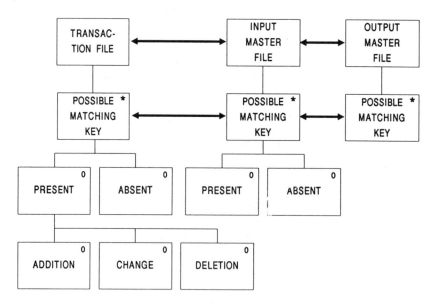

Figure 8.13

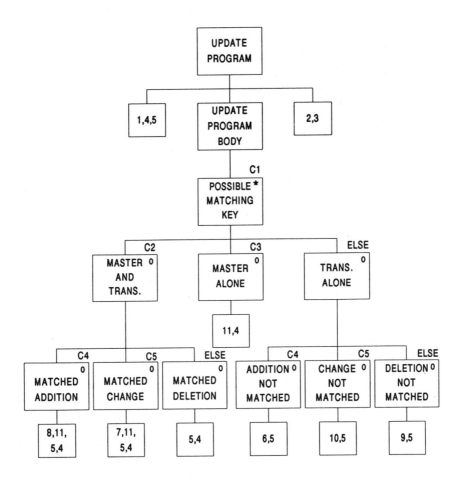

Figure 8.14

By combining the data structures, as we did in section 8.1, and noting that we are not interested in the condition 'transaction file record absent and input master record absent', we arrive at the program structure shown in figure 8.14.

Notice how the components of the transaction file that are part of PRESENT are repeated in the program structure for each of the selection parts that include 'transaction present'.

The above example demonstrates the principles of the sequential file update when there is, at most, one transaction per master file record.

The allocated conditions and operations for figure 8.14 are:

C1	Until end of both input files
C2	If master key = transaction key
C3	If master key < transaction key
C4	If transaction type = 'addition'
C5	If transaction type = 'change'
1	Open files
2	Close files
3	Stop
4	Read a master record
5	Read a transaction record
6	Write a new master record
7	Change an existing record and write to output
8	Display 'error - addition for existing record'
9	Display 'error - delete for non-existent record'
10	Display 'error - change for non-existent record'
11	Write unchanged master record to output

Let us now consider a problem where there is more than one transaction record for a given key.

In a simple stock control system, a sequential master file is maintained with one record for each product in stock. The products are identified by a stock number. A transaction file is applied to the master file at the end of each day and a new carried forward master file is produced. The transaction file records are of two types: (a) change the description of the product; and (b) change the quantity. There may be more than one transaction record for any given stock number. An error message is displayed for each transaction record without a corresponding master file record. The data structures for this problem are given in figure 8.15.

Combining at the points of correspondence and remembering the principles from our previous examples gives us the program structure of figure 8.16, to which we have added appropriate operations and conditions.

Note that the components DESCRIP. ALONE and QUANTITY ALONE have the same allocated operations. One could optimise this by removing these components and making TRANS. RECORD ALONE an elementary component with the allocated operations 8 and 5. Optimisation of this kind will simplify the structure, but it will also make it more difficult to amend. For instance, if we were later required to display a particular error message for an unmatched description transaction, we would have to restore the components that we removed.

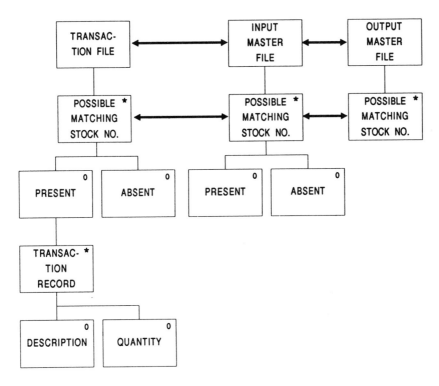

Figure 8.15

The conditions and operations for figure 8.16 are:

C1	Until end of both input files
C2	If master stock number = transaction stock number
C3	If master stock number < transaction stock number
C4	Until change of transaction stock number
C5	If transaction type = change of description
1	Open files
2	Close files
3	Stop
4	Read a master file record
5	Read a transaction file record
6	Write unchanged master record to output
7	Write amended master record to output
8	Display 'transaction alone' error message
9	Change master file record description
10	Change master file record quantity
11	Store transaction stock number

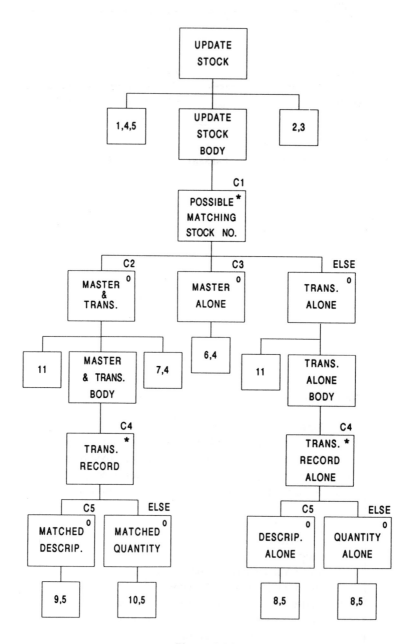

Figure 8.16

Of course, many sequential file updates are more complex than the above, essentially because of the complexity of the transaction file. For instance, a realistic transaction file would be sorted so that for any key the addition(s) come before the change(s) which come before the deletion(s). Also, second and subsequent additions and deletions for any key would give rise to an error.

8.4 Exercises

For each of the first three exercises you should:

(a) Produce logical data structures for the input files identical to figure 8.2 (though you should use component names appropriate to the problem), together with an output file structure.
(b) Combine the input data structures to produce a merged input structure with selection parts appropriate to the problem; then combine this structure with the output structure to produce a program structure.
(c) List conditions and elementary operations, then allocate them to the program structure, incorporating 'body' boxes as necessary.

You may assume in each case that the files are appropriately sorted.

8.4.1 A large used car sales organisation keeps a direct access file containing records of each car it has for sale. Included in the records are registration number, manufacturer and model. A second file is built up as cars are sold - the records in this file contain only registration number and date sold. Once weekly, the files are used to produce a list of descriptions (that is, manufacturer and model) of cars sold. Occasionally, there is a sale recorded without a corresponding description record being available, in which case 'description not known' is printed.

8.4.2 Two files are kept by Computa Training Limited. The first contains the names of all students who have been entered by Computa Training for the COBOL proficiency exam. The second contains the names of all students who have passed the exam. Not all students pass the exam and some may have been recorded as passed without being recorded as entered. It is required to produce an error report of those in this latter category, followed by the percentage pass rate of the correct records.

8.4.3 A CAL program for infants requires them to match each of a list of 26 words (each beginning with a different letter) with a set of 26 pictures. The pictures are flashed onto a VDU screen and the infant has 20 seconds to make the match. When the match is made, the picture is deleted from the picture file and the word from the word list file. The initial letter of the word is used as the key in each file. After 30 minutes the session is over and this leaves a number of picture records (which incidentally contain graphics details and the word that the picture represents) in one file, and a number of word records in another. The number of records in each should be the same, but due to a software bug, they are not.

To help the software design team to find the bug, you are required to produce the following:

(i) a list of initial letters of the words that have been deleted from both files, followed by

(ii) the percentage of picture file records remaining, followed by

(iii) the percentage of word file records remaining, followed by

(iv) the number of words with corresponding pictures that remain in the files.

8.4.4 A library records the following data when a book is borrowed, returned or renewed:

❑ borrower's reference number (6 digits)

❑ the date (dd mm yy)

❑ the book catalogue number (8 chars)

❑ a code = 1 for loan; 2 for renewal; 3 for return

❑ the time (hh mm ss).

At the end of each day the data collected are sorted into ascending order of time of day within catalogue number. The sorted file is then used to update a sequential book master file containing records as follows:

❑ book catalogue number (the sort key)

❑ date

❑ by whom borrowed (reference number) if applicable.

If the transaction code = 1, the date and the borrower's reference are changed in the master file record. If the transaction code = 2, the date only is changed. If the transaction code = 3, the borrower's reference in the master file is filled with spaces. There may be more than one transaction per book.

The only error situation to be considered is when a transaction record does not match a master record. This should be reported by a simple displayed message.

You are required to design a program to update the book status master file. Go through each stage from logical data structures to a program structure with allocated operations and conditions.

9 Structure Clashes and Inversion

9.1 Types of structure clash

We briefly mentioned the idea of structure clashes at the end of chapter 4. Structure clashes occur when it is not possible to combine logical data structures to produce a single program structure, because the logical data structures contradict or clash with each other.

There are, in fact, three different types of structure clash to consider - and resolve:

> (a) ordering clash
> (b) boundary clash
> (c) interleaving clash.

In this chapter we will describe each of the three different types, how and why they arise, and a method of solution in each case.

9.2 Ordering clash

A company keeps an expenditure file sorted by department. If it was required to produce a list of all items costing more than £100 in ascending order of cost, irrespective of department, we would create the data structures shown in figure 9.1.

Although the set of items represented by HIGH COST is identical to the set of items represented by HIGH COST ITEM, the items are not in the same order and hence we cannot draw a correspondence between them. Consequently, we cannot combine the structures to produce a single program structure.

However, we could resolve the clash by sorting the expenditure file into strict order of item cost only, and use the sorted file as input to a program to extract the high cost items as required. This solution is shown in figure 9.2.

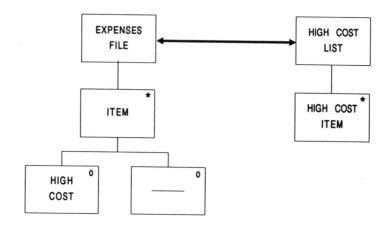

Figure 9.1

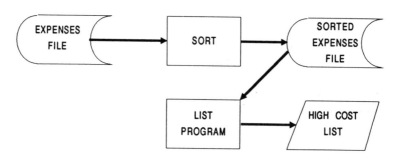

Figure 9.2

9.3 Boundary clash

9.3.1 Why boundary clashes occur

Suppose we are to produce a print program in which variable length blocks of information are to be printed about cars, one for each model in a car details file. Each block has a car make and model, followed by a variable number of print lines. The pages are to be numbered, and the car make and model are to be repeated at the head of a page when a block is split over more than one page. The print file has effectively two structures: the structure of the physical medium on which it is written (the printed page), and the structure of the data to be written (the grouping of lines by car model). Both of these structures must be taken into account. But, ignoring headings for the sake of simplicity, this gives us the situation shown in figure 9.3.

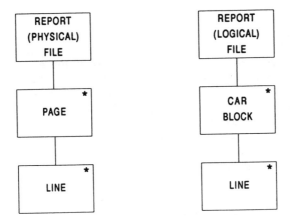

Figure 9.3

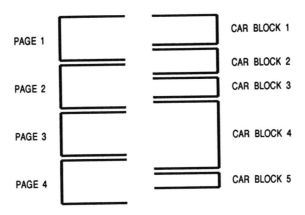

Figure 9.4

The difficulty is that a car block may be entirely contained within one page or may be split between pages - see figure 9.4.

Obviously we cannot draw a correspondence beween PAGE and CAR BLOCK. Furthermore, we cannot regard PAGE as an iteration of CAR BLOCK, or CAR BLOCK as an iteration of PAGE. Neither represents the relationship between pages and car blocks, since the boundary of a page clashes with the boundary of a car block.

Thus, we cannot produce a logical data structure for the report file that contains both the components PAGE and CAR BLOCK.

9.3.2 A typical example

A student file contains marks sorted by course. We are required to produce
a report which is split into pages, with a heading on each page. Student
names and marks are to be listed with totals at the end of each course.
There is no relationship between course and page. We could have a number
of courses per page (and several total lines) or a course could be spread
over a number of pages. We cannot ignore the division of the input file into
courses (because we are to produce totals at the end of each course), and
we cannot ignore the division of the output file into pages (because we are
to produce headings at the beginning of each page).

The appropriate data structures are shown in figure 9.5.

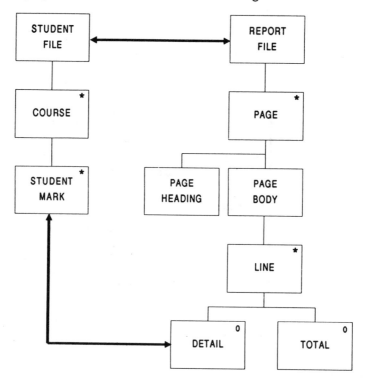

Figure 9.5

In producing the logical data structure for the report file, we have the
same problem with the components PAGE and COURSE as we identified at
the end of section 9.3.1. Having retained the component PAGE, we are
unable to include COURSE as a component. We attempt to overcome this
problem by means of a selection - each line on the page is either a detail
line or a course total line.

Obviously STUDENT FILE corresponds with REPORT FILE and STU-DENT MARK corresponds with DETAIL. But, COURSE does not correspond with PAGE and we cannot regard one as an iteration of the other. The boundary of COURSE clashes with the boundary of PAGE. Clearly we are not going to be able to combine them to produce a program structure. However, there is a solution to the problem.

9.4 Solving the boundary clash

First, notice how we overcame the ordering clash (figure 9.2). In creating the intermediate file, SORTED EXPENSES FILE, we have, in effect, solved two simpler problems. We can use a similar approach when faced with the more difficult problem of a boundary clash.

Consider the student marks problem above. There would be no difficulty in creating a program which read the student file and simply produced detail lines of print and, at appropriate points, course totals (that is, we did not have the complication of page boundaries).

The data structures and resultant program structure are given in figure 9.6.

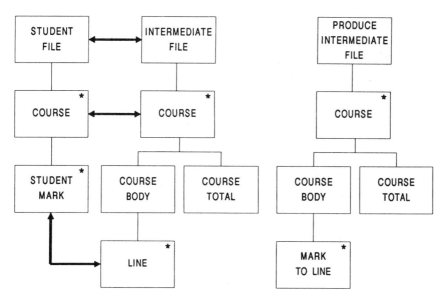

Figure 9.6

Similarly, if we had an intermediate file consisting simply of lines of print (detail lines interspersed at appropriate points by total lines), we would have little difficulty in producing the report file complete with page headings from it. The data structures are shown in figure 9.7.

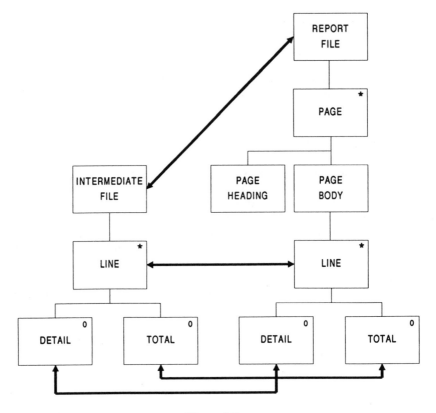

Figure 9.7

These give the program structure shown in figure 9.8.

So, we have solved two smaller problems and we can connect them as shown in figure 9.9.

Because we have both to write to and read from the intermediate file, perhaps this is not the most efficient solution from a processing point of view. But, the structures that we have produced are correct and maintainable, and there is a technique called program inversion which gets rid of the need for the intermediate file.

Obviously, there is only one physical intermediate file. However, as this example illustrates, the logical data structures for this file may vary, depending on whether it is viewed as the output (as in the first program) or the input (as in the second program).

We can now complete the design of the two programs separately by listing the conditions and operations, allocating them to the program structure and then producing schematic logic.

As we shall eventually replace the input and output (I/O) operations for the intermediate file by 'logical I/O operations', they have to be clearly identified. Therefore, in the first program, instead of just one operation

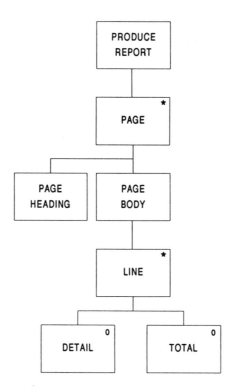

Figure 9.8

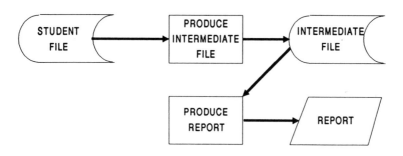

Figure 9.9

'open files', we use two separate operations for student file and intermediate file and similarly for 'close files'. In the second program we 'open'
and 'close' the intermediate file and report file separately.

Program 1 - produce an intermediate file from the student file (see figure 9.10)

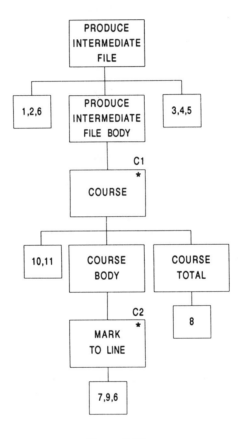

Figure 9.10

The condition list is:

C1	Until end of student file
C2	Until change of course or end of student file

The operation list is:

```
1    Open student file
2    Open intermediate file
3    Close student file
4    Close intermediate file
5    Stop
6    Read a student file record
7    Write intermediate file detail record
8    Write intermediate file total record
9    Accumulate course total
10   Initialise course total
11   Store course code
```

Now the schematic logic is shown in figure 9.11.

```
PRODUCE INTERMEDIATE FILE SEQ [Program 1
  DO 1   [Open student file
  DO 2   [Open intermediate file
  DO 6   [Read a student file record
  PRODUCE INTERMEDIATE FILE BODY ITER UNTIL C1 [end of
                                                   student file]
    COURSE SEQ
      DO 10   [Initialise course total
      DO 11   [Store course code
      COURSE BODY ITER UNTIL C2   [change of course or end
                                      of student file
        MARK TO LINE
          DO 7   [Write intermediate file detail record
          DO 9   [Accumulate course total
          DO 6   [Read a student file record
        MARK TO LINE END
      COURSE BODY END
      COURSE TOTAL
        DO 8   [Write intermediate file total record
      COURSE TOTAL END
    COURSE END
  PRODUCE INTERMEDIATE FILE BODY END
  DO 3   [Close student file
  DO 4   [Close intermediate file
  DO 5   [Stop
PRODUCE INTERMEDIATE FILE END
```

Figure 9.11

Program 2 - produce report file from the intermediate file (see figure 9.12)

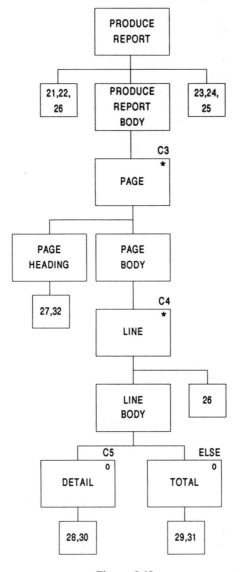

Figure 9.12

The condition list is:

C3	Until end of intermediate file
C4	Until end of page or end of intermediate file
C5	If a detail line

The operation list is:

21	Open intermediate file
22	Open report file
23	Close report file
24	Close intermediate file
25	Stop
26	Read an intermediate file record
27	Print page headings
28	Print a detail line
29	Print a total line
30	Increment line count by 1
31	Increment line count by 4
32	Initialise line count

The schematic logic is as shown in figure 9.13.

```
PRODUCE REPORT SEQ [Program 2
  DO 21 [Open intermediate file
  DO 22 [Open report file
  DO 26 [Read an intermediate file record
  PRODUCE REPORT BODY ITER UNTIL C3 [end of intermediate file
    PAGE SEQ
      PAGE HEADING
        DO 27 [Print page headings
        DO 32 [Initialise line count
      PAGE HEADING END
      PAGE BODY ITER UNTIL C4 [end of page or end of
                                        intermediate file
        LINE SEQ
          LINE BODY SEL IF C5 [detail line
            DETAIL
              DO 28 [Print a detail line
              DO 30 [Increment line count by 1
            DETAIL END
          LINE BODY ELSE 1
            TOTAL
              DO 29 [Print a total line
              DO 31 [Increment line count by 4
            TOTAL END
          LINE BODY END
          DO 26 [Read an intermediate file record
        LINE END
      PAGE BODY END
    PAGE END
  PRODUCE REPORT BODY END
  DO 23 [Close report file
  DO 24 [Close intermediate file
  DO 25 [Stop
PRODUCE REPORT END
```

Figure 9.13

9.5 Program inversion

The intermediate file is a serial file. This means that when writing, the records are written one after another as they are produced; and on reading, the records are read in the same order in which they have been written.

If the two programs that write and read the intermediate file were executed at the same time, theoretically, once a record was written by the first program, it could be read by the second program. We could represent this diagrammatically as shown in figure 9.14.

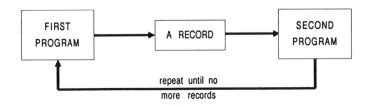

Figure 9.14

A practical method of achieving this is to combine the two programs by making one a subprogram (subroutine or procedure) of the other, with an intermediate file record being passed from the main program to the subprogram (or vice versa). Thus we no longer need a physical intermediate file since only one record is active at any one time. This means that the operations for the intermediate file (open, close, read and write) have to be replaced by 'logical I/O operations'. In effect, as we shall see later, instead of writing to the intermediate file, we pass the intermediate file record to the subprogram as a parameter. Then, instead of reading from the intermediate file, we exit to the main program to obtain another record.

We can summarise the 'rules' for program inversion as follows:

1. Decide on the most appropriate inversion (that is, which program should be the subprogram).
2. Identify the I/O operations for the intermediate file as 'logical I/O operations'.
3. Apply specific rules for the implementation of the 'logical I/O operations' at the coding stage.

The way in which we remove the intermediate file and make one program a subprogram called by the other is now demonstrated in detail.

We will choose to make the second program a subroutine of the first. Coding from the schematic logic may now be done with specific rules for the identified 'logical I/O operations'.

First, the main program (program 1). Instead of writing to the intermediate file, we are going to call the subroutine and pass an intermediate file record together with an intermediate file status indicator, which indicates when the file is open or closed (in order to implement 'end of intermediate file' for conditions C3 and C4 in the subprogram).

We code

```
2    Open intermediate file
```

by initialising an intermediate file status indicator.

In COBOL,

```
MOVE O TO INTER-EOF.
```

In Pascal,

```
inter_eof := FALSE ;
```

We code

```
7    Write intermediate file detail record
```

by calling the subroutine and making available the intermediate file record and the intermediate file status indicator. The type of intermediate file record (detail or total) must also be conveyed to the subroutine. For illustrative purposes, we will make these available by parameter passing in COBOL and using global areas in Pascal.

In COBOL,

```
MOVE "D" TO D-REC-TYPE.
MOVE COURSE-CODE TO D-COURSE.
MOVE NAME TO D-NAME.
MOVE MARK TO D-MARK.
CALL REP-SR USING INTER-EOF DETAIL-RECORD.
```

In Pascal,

```
rectype := 'D' ;
Reportsr ;
```

We code

```
8    Write intermediate file total record
```

by calling the subprogram as above.

In COBOL,

```
MOVE "T" TO T-REC-TYPE.
MOVE STORED-COURSE TO T-COURSE.
MOVE COURSE-TOT TO T-TOTAL.
CALL REP-SR USING INTER-EOF TOTAL-RECORD.
```

In Pascal,

```
rectype := 'T' ;
Reportsr ;
```

We code

```
4    Close intermediate file
```

by calling the subprogram as above, except that the intermediate file status indicator is set to 'end of file' and the intermediate file record contents are irrelevant.

In COBOL,

```
MOVE 1 TO INTER-EOF.
CALL REP-SR USING INTER-EOF NULL-RECORD.
```

In Pascal,

```
inter_eof := TRUE ;
Reportsr ;
```

Now the coding for the subprogram (program 2). For a 'logical read' of the intermediate file we exit to the main program to obtain an intermediate file record. In order to maintain continuity within the subprogram, on re-entry, we must ensure that the subprogram is executed from the instruction after the appropriate 'read'. This means inserting labels at each point of exit, and right at the beginning of the subprogram including a statement which will transfer control to the point in the code from where we last exited.

In COBOL,

```
     GOTO ENTRY-1 ENTRY-2......ENTRY-n
        DEPENDING ON ENTRY-STATUS.
ENTRY-1.
```

There will be the same number of ENTRY-n labels as read intermediate file statements (that is, 2 in our case). ENTRY-STATUS is a WORKING-STORAGE entry in the subprogram, with an initial value of one.

In Pascal,

```
    IF entrystatus = 1 THEN GOTO 10
    ELSE IF entrystatus = 2 THEN GOTO 20
    ELSE IF entrystatus = n THEN GOTO n0 ;
10:
```

where 10, 20, n0 are declared as labels. **entrystatus** is an integer variable initialised to 1 at the start of the main program.

We code

```
21   Open intermediate file
```

and the first occurrence of

```
26   Read an intermediate file record
```

by nothing!! This is because the first call of the subroutine passes the first intermediate file record.

We code the second and subsequent occurrences of

```
26   Read an intermediate file record
```

by setting the entry status indicator to a value that indicates which occurrence of the 'read' it is (that is, for the second read use value 2, for the third use 3 etc.); then exiting from the subprogram (or passing control to a common exit point); then inserting a label to correspond to the entry point handling code mentioned above.

In COBOL,

```
    MOVE 2 TO ENTRY-STATUS.
    EXIT PROGRAM.
ENTRY-2.
```

In Pascal,

```
    entrystatus := 2 ;
    GOTO 9999 ;
20:
```

where the label 9999 is situated as a common exit point from the subprogram (procedure).

We code

24	Close intermediate file

by nothing!!
  We replace

25	Stop

by code to exit from the subprogram:
  In COBOL,

```
EXIT PROGRAM.
```

In Pascal, this is not applicable.

We code

end of intermediate file in C3 and C4

by testing the value of the intermediate file status indicator.

A full implementation of this boundary clash solution is given in both languages in appendix J.

The coding rules given above are now summarised in figure 9.15. You may find it beneficial to re-examine the rules in the light of this diagram.

In the above example we overcame the structure clash by creating an intermediate file of LINES (that is, using one LINE per intermediate file record). There was no point in using a record larger than LINE (such as PAGE), since that would not remove the clash. If the clashing logical data structures had contained an entity smaller than LINE (for example, FIELD or CHARACTER) in addition to LINE, then creating an intermediate file of this entity would have removed the clash, but would obviously be inefficient. In general, we create an intermediate file of the largest entity common to the clashing structures (that is, the highest level non-clashing component).

We have explained the technique of inversion by providing coding rules that can be applied directly to the schematic logic of the two programs. However, when developing such programs, it is recommended that you initially code the two programs separately (that is, without using subprograms); test program 1 to create the intermediate file, then test program 2 using this intermediate file as input; then, once the two programs are correct, apply the coding rules to remove the intermediate file by making program 2 a subprogram of program 1.

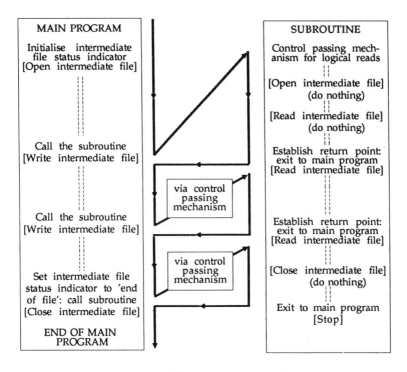

Figure 9.15

As exercises 9.7.1 and 9.7.2 relate to the boundary clash and program inversion, you may attempt them at this stage, before considering the interleaving clash.

9.6 Interleaving clash

Consider a multiprogramming computer which runs a number of jobs (each containing a number of programs) simultaneously. We could show the schedule with a simple bar chart like that shown in figure 9.16.

Suppose the computer logged the start and finish of the jobs and the programs, then the data would be as shown in figure 9.17.

If we attempt to process the data (log file) to produce details of elapsed time per job and per program, we find that the structure of the log file just does not represent job or program entities. The entities that we want are interleaved; the only way we can draw a logical data structure is to show that the logging file records are either job starts, job ends, program starts or program ends. So, we have the structures given in figure 9.18.

The structure clash is clear. LOG FILE corresponds with LOG ANALYSIS,

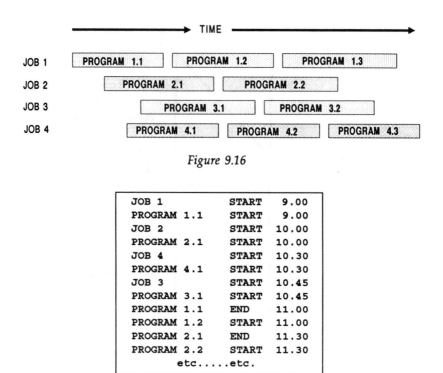

Figure 9.16

Figure 9.17

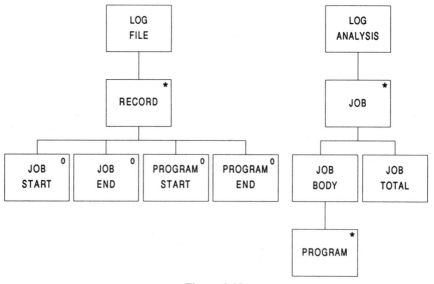

Figure 9.18

but further correspondences are impossible. One solution is perhaps obvious - if we sort the log file into program within job order, we have no problems. But what if there is no time to sort or if we want a continuous analysis throughout the day? We must apply another solution.

Program inversion can be applied to solve the problem. Essentially, the solution is the same as that outlined for the boundary clash problem above, except that we have more than one intermediate file (that is, one per job). The first program simply creates a new file for each new job and writes each record from the log file to the appropriate job file. The second program reads each job file in turn and produces the analysis. Of course, one needs to keep track of all the files created and if the number of files is known to be small then the data could be kept in store. The technique of program inversion allows us to combine the two programs into one, thus allowing immediate production of analysis data as soon as all data for a job are assembled.

9.7 Exercises

9.7.1 In respect of the student marks problem (figures 9.11, 9.13 and appendix J), given the following data, show the contents of the entry status indicator, the intermediate file status indicator and the intermediate file record (or equivalent global data areas) for each occurrence of the operations affected by the coding rules (that is 2, 4, 7, 8, 21, 24, 25, 26).

Use a student file of the form:

```
MATHS    F JONES   35
MATHS    C DODD    48
SCIENCE  J BROWN   62
```

9.7.2 A stock file contains product detail records comprising: a product group code, a product code, the product description and the stock level. The file is sorted into product code within product group order. An example of the file contents is:

group	product code	description	stock level
A	1234	NUTS	25
A	1316	BOLTS	13
A	4312	SCREWS	46
C	1625	WOOD GLUE	15
C	2315	SUPER GLUE	29
D	1234	HAMMER	42
D	6678	CHISEL	32

A report is required of all products for which the stock level has fallen below the reserve level of 20. The report is to be paged with standard page headings (title, page number and date). In addition to the product details being printed (one per line), a total of the number of different products selected per product group is to be shown at the end of each group. There is no relationship between product group and page. There could be more than one product group per page, and a product group could span.more than one page. You may assume that there are no blank lines in the report.

Design a program to produce this report by following these steps:

(a) Draw logical data structures for the stock file and report, and then, as you attempt to find correspondences, you should identify a boundary clash.
(b) For program 1 (produce intermediate file from stock file), go through each stage from logical data structures to program structure with allocated operations and conditions.
(c) Repeat (b) for program 2 (produce report from intermediate file).
(d) Indicate how you would now remove the intermediate file by amending certain operations, including others and making one program a subprogram of the other.

9.7.3 Describe in your own words

(a) Why structure clashes occur.
(b) How program inversion aids the solution of structure clashes.

If you wish, you may now attempt the case study in appendix C.

10 Recognition Problems and Backtracking

10.1 Introduction

For most problems we can 'find our way' through the program structure by reading one record ahead. By inspecting the next record to be processed (that is, the record just read), we can determine whether or not there is a further occurrence of the iterated part of an iteration and which part of a selection is to be executed.

Sometimes, however, we need to read more than one record ahead. Consider a file of personnel details where for each person there is either one or two records - a financial record and/or a non-financial record. It is possible to have (for any person) either one of the records, or both records in either order. We have a structure as shown in figure 10.1.

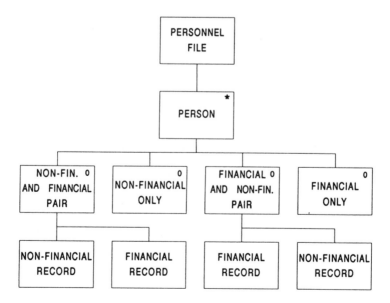

Figure 10.1

The problem with this structure is that we cannot construct the conditions unless we have the next two records to be processed available for selection. So we introduce a two record read ahead.

A simple two record read ahead routine might be:

```
Copy area-2 into area-1
If not end of file
    read a record into area-2
```

This routine would be performed for every record required. That is, it would be performed twice at the beginning and when two records have been processed, and once when one record has been processed.

Now consider the problem of validating a transaction file containing batches of records. Each batch contains a number of detail records followed by a batch total record. Each record is of fixed length containing a batch number, a code, an amount and the type (detail or total). The amount in the total record is the sum of each detail record (but it could be wrong). The code in the total record is always zeros and does not need validating, but the code in the detail records should be within a specific range. The validation rules state that batches without errors are written to an accepted batches file, and batches with errors are written to a rejected batches file. Also, the computed batch total amount for an accepted batch is displayed at the operator's terminal.

In drawing a logical data structure for the transaction file, we must distinguish between an accepted batch and a rejected batch. For an accepted batch we include only components relevant to the processing of an accepted batch; for example, the computed total is displayed only for an accepted batch. For a rejected batch we include only components relevant to the treatment of a batch known to contain errors; thus there is no need to distinguish between detail records and total records for a rejected batch, assuming that we can use the same write operation for both. The structure will not contain a selection component of valid or invalid record depending on code, because the accepted batch will contain only valid records and the rejected batch processing for this problem does not need to distinguish between the valid and invalid records. For the same reason, we do not include a selection component of correct or incorrect batch total record.

The data structure for the transaction file is as shown in figure 10.2.

The problem here is that we cannot evaluate the condition for ACCEPTED BATCH until we have processed the whole batch. The solution would appear to be a multiple record read ahead. But how many records do we read?

A more practical solution is found in the technique of backtracking. It must be stressed, however, that the structures for ACCEPTED BATCH and REJECTED BATCH would still be produced on the 'assumption' that we could evaluate the condition.

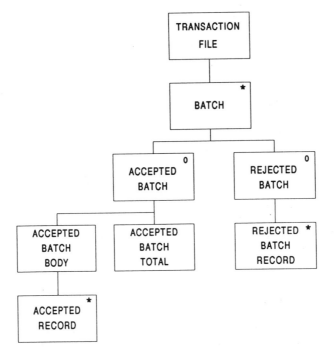

Figure 10.2

10.2 The technique of backtracking

In general, this technique may be applied where we have recognition problems. That is, when the natural and correct program structure cannot be directly implemented because of an inability to evaluate the controlling condition for one or more constructs. The solution to such problems is first described by means of an allegory.

Suppose we have two sets of playing cards which are placed face down on a table, and it is known that one set contains an ace (and no kings) and the other set a king (and no aces). How do we select the one with the ace? We cannot know which to select, so we make an arbitrary choice and examine the selected set, one card at a time, until we find the ace (we have made the right choice!) or we find the king (we have made the wrong choice!). In the latter case we now pick up the second set and, if necessary, re-arrange the first set as if it had not been disturbed.

If we cannot make a decision at the outset, then we adopt the following procedure:

1. Make an arbitrary choice (or an informed guess if there are some clues) assuming it to be the correct one. We call this a POSIT.

2. Follow up that choice until such time as it is proved to be right or wrong.
3. If the choice is found to be incorrect, then stop following the choice made (we call this a QUIT) and follow instead the alternative choice (this is called an ADMIT).
4. If by taking the wrong choice we have disturbed something, we must identify the importance of this disturbance. We call such disturbances SIDE EFFECTS.
5. A side effect may be intolerable; for example, we should not have disturbed the first set of cards.
6. Or a side effect may be neutral (or tolerable); for example, it does not matter that we have disturbed the first set of cards.
7. Or a side effect may be favourable; for example, we needed to move the first set of cards anyway.
8. For the intolerable side effects, we make arrangements to reverse them; for example, replace the first set in exactly the same place and order.

10.3 The accepted and rejected batch problem

Let us now apply the above technique to the accepted and rejected batch problem introduced in section 10.1. The input data structure is given in figure 10.2.

The output structures are 'accepted file', an iteration of 'accepted batch' whose structure is given by the component ACCEPTED BATCH in figure 10.2; and 'rejected file', an iteration of 'rejected batch' whose structure is given by the component REJECTED BATCH also in figure 10.2. The correspondences being obvious, we arrive at the program structure shown in figure 10.3 with allocated operations and conditions.

The conditions and operations are:

C1	Until end of file
C2	If a valid (accepted) batch !!!
C3	Until end of batch record (that is, total record)
C4	Until change of batch or end of file
1	Open files
2	Close files
3	Stop
4	Read a transaction file record
5	Write transaction record to accepted file
6	Display computed batch total
7	Write transaction record to rejected file
8	Add amount to batch total
9	Initialise batch total
10	Store batch number

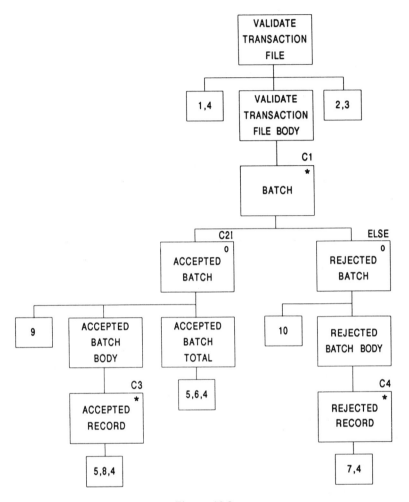

Figure 10.3

We now continue with the design process and produce schematic logic, omitting the reference to condition C2. This gives the schematic logic shown in figure 10.4.

Next we amend the schematic logic by adopting the following procedure. (The modified schematic logic is given in figure 10.5.)

(a) Replace the BATCH SEL by BATCH POSIT.

(b) Replace the BATCH ELSE 1 by BATCH ADMIT.

(c) Identify the points in the accepted batch procedures where it may become known that the batch is invalid and insert QUIT statements.

```
VALIDATE TRANSACTION FILE SEQ
  DO 1  [Open files
  DO 4  [Read a transaction file record
  VALIDATE TRANSACTION FILE BODY ITER UNTIL C1 [end of file
    BATCH SEL
      ACCEPTED BATCH SEQ
        DO 9  [Initialise batch total
        ACCEPTED BATCH BODY ITER UNTIL C3 [end of batch record
          ACCEPTED RECORD
            DO 5  [Write transaction record to accepted file
            DO 8  [Add amount to batch total
            DO 4  [Read a transaction file record
          ACCEPTED RECORD END
        ACCEPTED BATCH BODY END
        ACCEPTED BATCH TOTAL
            DO 5  [Write transaction record to accepted file
            DO 6  [Display computed batch total
            DO 4  [Read a transaction file record
        ACCEPTED BATCH TOTAL END
      ACCEPTED BATCH END
    BATCH ELSE 1
      REJECTED BATCH SEQ
        DO 10  [Store batch number
        REJECTED BATCH BODY ITER UNTIL C4 [change of batch or
                                             end of file
          REJECTED RECORD
            DO 7  [Write transaction record to rejected file
            DO 4  [Read a transaction file record
          REJECTED RECORD END
        REJECTED BATCH BODY END
      REJECTED BATCH END
    BATCH END
  VALIDATE TRANSACTION FILE BODY END
  DO 2  [Close files
  DO 3  [Stop
VALIDATE TRANSACTION FILE END
```

Figure 10.4

Two QUITs from BATCH POSIT are necessary:

(i) If the code in a detail record is invalid (not in range).
(ii) If the computed batch total is not equal to the total in the batch total record.

We insert the first at the beginning of ACCEPTED RECORD, and the second at the beginning of ACCEPTED BATCH TOTAL. The conditions for the QUITs are added to the condition list:

C5 If invalid code
C6 If computed total not = total in the batch total record

(Occasionally, though not in this case, it may be necessary to support a condition by including additional operations before a QUIT.)

(d) Identify and classify side effects. We look at all operations in the ACCEPTED BATCH process that come logically before the last QUIT. Hence:

(i) Operation 9 [Initialise batch total] is a neutral side effect.

(ii) Operation 5 [Write transaction record to accepted file], in ACCEPTED RECORD, is an intolerable side effect because, if the batch turns out to be a rejected one, none of its records should be written to the accepted file.

(iii) Operation 8 [Add amount to batch total] is a neutral side effect because although it is unnecessary to the REJECTED BATCH process, it will not interfere with it, and anyway its effects are cancelled at the beginning of a new batch.

(iv) Operation 4 [Read a transaction file record], after operation 8, is an intolerable side effect because a read statement for a serial or sequential file advances past the last record read, and it is necessary to process the records in a rejected batch from the beginning of the batch.

(e) Insert operations to overcome the intolerable side effects (see ** in figure 10.5).

For (ii) above, we need to postpone the output to the accepted file by writing it to a temporary file. This means

11   Initialise temporary file (reset to beginning if necessary)

is allocated right at the beginning of BATCH POSIT.
The first operation 5 becomes

5A   Write transaction record to temporary file

Then

12   Copy temporary file contents to accepted file

is included immediately after the last QUIT.
(The coding of operation 11 must allow for the situation where the temporary file has remained open owing to a prior quit from the accepted batch process.)

For (iv) we need to undo the reading of the transaction file by repositioning to the beginning of the current batch. This means

13	Store position of start of the batch

is allocated at the beginning of BATCH POSIT, and

14	Reposition the transaction file to start of the current batch

is allocated right at the beginning of BATCH ADMIT.

In this particular problem both the 'read' and 'write' are intolerable side effects. This is not always the case as you will see later from exercise 10.7.1 and case study D.

10.4 Dealing with intolerable side effects

Having classified the side effects as favourable, neutral or intolerable by examining each operation of the POSIT which comes logically before the last QUIT, we must overcome the intolerable side effects. We shall now summarise the main techniques.

Consider the situation where POSIT processing may change the state of certain variables, but ADMIT needs the original states. This can be catered for by storing (or freezing) the state of computation on entry to the POSIT, and retrieving (or unfreezing) on entry to the ADMIT. For example, on entry to POSIT we may store a copy of the contents of all variables whose state is (or may be) changed by POSIT processing; then if the ADMIT component is entered, the values would be retrieved from the temporary copy area.

Serial access read operations in the POSIT can give rise to intolerable side effects (for example, 'read a transaction file record' in the problem of section 10.3) as ADMIT may need to access the records read past. This can be overcome, as indicated in section 10.3, by storing the position of the file at the beginning of the POSIT and then repositioning the file to the stored position right at the beginning of the ADMIT.

The basic principle employed in both the above situations is the same - store at the start of POSIT and retrieve at the start of ADMIT.

Output operations in the POSIT can also lead to intolerable side effects. As we saw in section 10.3, the first occurrence of 'write transaction record to accepted file' was intolerable, because if the batch turns out to be a rejected one, none of its records should be written to the accepted file. We therefore replaced the above write by 'write transaction record to temporary

```
VALIDATE TRANSACTION FILE SEQ
  DO 1  [Open files
  DO 4  [Read a transaction file record
  VALIDATE TRANSACTION FILE BODY ITER UNTIL C1 [end of file
    BATCH POSIT (Batch is an accepted batch)
      DO 11  [Initialise temporary file                      **
      DO 13  [Store position of start of the batch           **
      ACCEPTED BATCH SEQ
        DO 9  [Initialise batch total
        ACCEPTED BATCH BODY ITER UNTIL C3 [end of batch record
          ACCEPTED RECORD
            QUIT BATCH POSIT IF C5 [invalid code
            DO 5A [Write transaction record to temporary file **
            DO 8  [Add amount to batch total
            DO 4  [Read a transaction file record
          ACCEPTED RECORD END
        ACCEPTED BATCH BODY END
        ACCEPTED BATCH TOTAL
          QUIT BATCH POSIT IF C6 [computed total <> total in the
                                  batch total record
          DO 12 [Copy temporary file contents to accepted file**
          DO 5  [Write transaction record to accepted file
          DO 6  [Display computed batch total
          DO 4  [Read a transaction file record
        ACCEPTED BATCH TOTAL END
      ACCEPTED BATCH END
    BATCH ADMIT (Batch is not accepted)
      DO 14  [Reposition the transaction file to the start of
              the current batch                              **
      REJECTED BATCH SEQ
        DO 10  [Store batch number
        REJECTED BATCH BODY ITER UNTIL C4 [change of batch or
                                           end of file
          REJECTED RECORD
            DO 7  [Write transaction record to rejected file
            DO 4  [Read a transaction file record
          REJECTED RECORD END
        REJECTED BATCH BODY END
      REJECTED BATCH END
    BATCH END
  VALIDATE TRANSACTION FILE BODY END
  DO 2  [Close files
  DO 3  [Stop
VALIDATE TRANSACTION FILE END
```

Figure 10.5

file' and then copied the contents of the temporary file to the accepted file immediately after the last QUIT.

In the batch problem, a file has to be used as the temporary storage area, because we do not know the size of the batch. Obviously, the precise form of this temporary area (or buffer) will depend on the data being held. In some cases a few records or an array might suffice.

POSIT and ADMIT processing may output to different files (as in the batch problem) or require different output to the same file. In all cases the basic principle remains the same - we do not execute the write statement at the point indicated in the POSIT, but postpone the output until all QUIT points have been passed.

10.5 Implementing quits

We shall now consider another typical validation situation, which would normally be part of a larger problem, and then illustrate the coding required for QUITs.

A record has three fields: a code, a type and a part number. The record is valid if, and only if, all three fields are valid. The structure of the record can be shown simply as in figure 10.6.

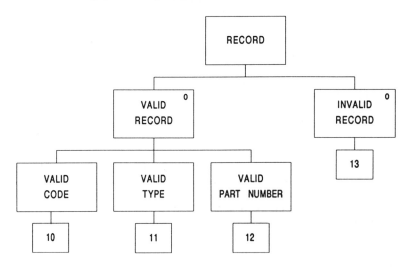

Figure 10.6

This structure shows clearly that we are interested in only two possibilities. The record is either valid or it is invalid. If it is invalid, we wish to regard it merely as a bad or rejected record. If it is valid we wish to process the fields code, type and part number in certain specific ways. What the structure does not show is that we cannot evaluate the selection between valid record and invalid record so simply. This is because the processing of the first field (code) establishes the conditions for validating the second field (type), and the processing of the second field establishes the conditions for validating the third field (part number). So we begin the processing of the record as if it were a valid record, and take steps to recognise at a later stage that what we may have is an invalid record.

Employing the POSIT/ADMIT construct we have the schematic logic as shown in figure 10.7 (note that elementary components have been omitted for clarity).

The COBOL coding for this example is given in figure 10.8. In Pascal, we might code the example as shown in figure 10.9.

Note the strictly controlled use of GOTO. For each QUIT we go to the ADMIT branch. At the end of the POSIT branch, we go to the end of the POSIT/ADMIT component.

```
RECORD POSIT (a valid record)
  VALID RECORD SEQ
    QUIT RECORD POSIT IF C1 [code is invalid
    DO 10 [Process code
    QUIT RECORD POSIT IF C2 [type is invalid
    DO 11 [Process type
    QUIT RECORD POSIT IF C3 [part number is invalid
    DO 12 [Process part number
  VALID RECORD END
RECORD ADMIT (an invalid record)
  DO 13 [Process error record
RECORD END
```

Figure 10.7

```
RECORD-POSIT.
VALID-RECORD-SEQ.
    IF CODE-ERROR GO TO RECORD-ADMIT.
    Process code
    IF TYPE-ERROR GO TO RECORD-ADMIT.
    Process type
    IF PART-NO-ERROR GO TO RECORD-ADMIT.
    Process part number
VALID-RECORD-END.
    GO TO RECORD-END.
RECORD-ADMIT.
    Process error record
RECORD-END.
```

Figure 10.8

```
LABEL 30,40 ;

    (* record posit - a valid record *)
       (* valid record seq *)
          IF code_error THEN GOTO 30 ;
          Process code
          IF type_error THEN GOTO 30 ;
          Process type
          IF part_no_error THEN GOTO 30 ;
          Process part number
       (* valid record end *)
       GOTO 40;
30: (* record admit - an invalid record *)
    Process error record
40: (* record end *)
```

Figure 10.9

10.6 Quit from iteration

If necessary, the QUIT statement can be introduced into the iteration construct. The ordinary form of iteration imposes the constraint that the terminating condition must be capable of evaluation at the head of the loop. In some situations this cannot be satisfied without introducing switches, which inevitably makes the structure more complex. There may be several circumstances under which the iteration is to be terminated, and they may not all be capable of evaluation at the head of the loop. In some processes, some of the processing within the iteration component must be completed before exiting, or some of the processing may be necessary for elaboration of the terminating condition. We therefore introduce the QUIT statement into the iteration construct.

The condition is normally removed from the head of the iteration and

      QUIT COMPONENT-NAME ITER

or

      QUIT COMPONENT-NAME ITER IF CN [terminating condition

is then included at the appropriate place within the iterated component. In the first case, the effect is to transfer control to the end of the iteration unconditionally; in the second case, control is passed to the end of the iteration when the condition is true.

We consider an application of QUIT from iteration in chapter 12 when dealing with one of the possible implementations for an iteration of at least one occurrence - the iterated component must be executed in order to establish the terminating condition.

10.7 Exercise

10.7.1 A chain store file contains records, each containing a department code, record type indicator and other fields. A type 1 record contains the start-of-day cash figure; a type 2 record the end-of-day cash figure. A program is required that will detect errors and store correct data in an accepted file. If the data for a department are valid, they are written to the accepted file; if invalid in any way, the data are rejected and the following message is displayed:

INCORRECT DATA FOR DEPARTMENT nnnnnn

Data for a department are valid if:

(i) There are exactly 2 records for the department, a type 1 and a type 2 record, in that order.
(ii) The value of both cash fields is in the range £100 to £100,000.
(iii) The value of cash at the end of day on the type 2 record is strictly greater than the value of cash at the start of the day on the type 1 record.

The records are sorted into ascending order of record type indicator within department code.

Design the program to detect the above errors and produce appropriate output by following these steps:

(a) Construct logical data structures for
   ❏ the chain store file
   ❏ the accepted file.
(b) Identify correspondences and produce a program structure.
(c) List the elementary operations and conditions.
(d) Allocate these to the program structure.
(e) Revise the program structure to include body boxes, if necessary.
(f) Produce schematic logic.
(g) Revise the schematic logic to introduce as appropriate POSIT, ADMIT and QUIT.
(h) Classify any side effects.
(i) Amend the operation list and condition list to cater for side effect processing and QUITs.
(j) Revise the schematic logic to incorporate side effect processing.

If you wish, you may now attempt the case study in appendix D.

11 Procedurisation

11.1 Introduction

We shall use the term 'procedure' in a general sense to include those parts of a complete program variously called subprograms, functions, subroutines and segments. In general, procedurisation is used to break the problem down into more manageable parts to facilitate detail design, testing and maintenance. However, the programmer is often faced with the dilemma of deciding which parts to procedurise. In addition to run-time overheads and the problems of interfacing, the ill-advised use of procedures can lead to implementation and maintenance problems rather than reducing them. The programmer should therefore always have sound reasons for procedurising and, in doing so, should ensure that the principles of JSP are not contradicted. For example, in chapter 9 we used a subprogram, with good reason, to solve the structure clash problem by considering two simpler problems instead. The purpose of this chapter is to provide some general guidelines on procedurisation within the context of JSP.

11.2 Bottom-up procedures

A programmer should be aware of and make use of, with due consideration for portability, the available facilities (such as string handling routines, sort procedures etc.), whether these are provided by the programming language or a library. However, if the base design level, as defined by the facilities of the target language and the available library routines, does not contain the required operations or data structures, then such facilities can be created. Procedures created in this way are often termed 'bottom-up' procedures. The decision to use them could be made on inspection of the problem specification (that is, before data structures are produced).

For example, suppose it is required to produce a piece of software based on the processing of days of the week. Irrespective of the overall task to be accomplished, it could be decided that the following basic facilities are needed:

(a) A data structure to represent days of the week.

(b) Routines for the input, output and comparison of the days of the week.

Given that these facilities are not present in the target language, they would have to be constructed. Thus, the base level is raised in the sense that 'write day of the week', for example, could then be regarded as an elementary operation and coded by a procedure call.

11.3 Top-down procedures

Consider the fragment shown in figure 11.1 from a program structure.

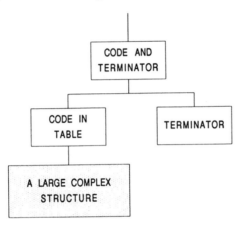

Figure 11.1

If we assume that CODE IN TABLE is large or complex, then the program quality may be improved by making CODE IN TABLE a separate procedure. Such a decision could be made when developing the program structure, before operations and conditions are allocated.

This would mean:

1. Separating the structures, so that in effect CODE IN TABLE becomes an elementary component of the higher level structure, as shown in figure 11.2. Note that the references 3.4/CODE-SUB and 3.4/MAIN-PROG are used to link the two structures for documentation purposes.
2. When allocating operations,

12 Derive table code (say)

would be allocated to CODE IN TABLE.

3. At the coding stage this operation would then be coded by the procedure call.

Similarly, if the structure subordinate to TERMINATOR is large or

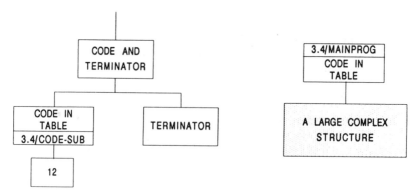

Figure 11.2

complex then this could also be procedurised. The purpose of such procedurisation is primarily to enhance readability. The overall process performed by the higher level structure (the calling procedure) should then be easily perceived without recourse to the detailed structures of the called procedures.

There are no parameters to procedures created in this way because they are dependent on program context in terms of both function and interface. Parameters would be artificial.

Let us now consider the example shown in figure 11.3.

We shall assume that the structures with allocated operations and conditions subordinate to both occurrences of TYPE 1 GROUP are non-trivial and identical. We can then avoid repetition of the same code, and hence reduce program size, by using a procedure for TYPE 1 GROUP. This is known as coding optimisation. Obviously, the decision to use procedures in this way can only be taken by inspecting the program structure with allocated operations and conditions. The procedure is implemented using the steps outlined in the previous example. Once again we have the advantage of enhanced readability. Similarly, if the structures with allocated operations and conditions subordinate to the components TYPE 2 GROUP were identical, then they could also be procedurised.

However, in making the decision to optimise on space, we must be aware of the consequences. Using the same procedure in two different contexts means that it may have to be parameterised. The program may also be more difficult to debug and modify. If an error occurs in such a procedure, unless we had detailed tracing information, we would not know from which part of the program it had been called. A minor modification to the program specification could mean that the structures subordinate to the components TYPE 1 GROUP were no longer identical, in which case the procedure could no longer be used. For this reason, if the decision to optimise is taken, one should always preserve the unoptimised design.

Let us now assume that the structure with allocated operations and conditions for TYPE 1 GROUP is similar, but not identical, to that for TYPE 2 GROUP. Some programmers may then be tempted to devise a general

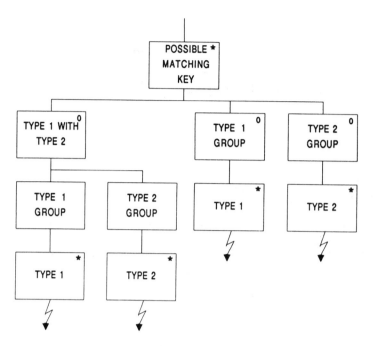

Figure 11.3

procedure which could be used for both TYPE 1 GROUP and TYPE 2 GROUP. This form of procedurisation is not recommended. The program code should always be derived from the program structure which, in turn, must be derived from the data structures. The program structure should never be modified merely to allow procedurisation to be used.

Finally, a word of warning. Problems can arise if procedures are used within programs involving inversion or backtracking. Both these techniques require the use of GOTO, but transferring control from one procedure to another invariably causes problems. The precise effect of such a jump can vary from one language to another; it may even vary between implementations of a particular language, and it may even depend on the type of procedure being used (for example, PERFORM or CALL in COBOL). It is not the intention therefore to discuss this problem in any depth, but merely to remind you that:

1. To maintain continuity within an inverted program, a statement is inserted at the beginning of the subprogram to transfer control to the point in the code from which we last exited (see chapter 9). If the subprogram is itself procedurised then this could mean jumping out of one procedure to the middle of another.
2. The QUIT in backtracking involves jumping from the POSIT to the ADMIT structure. If they are in separate procedures, then once again the results could be unpredictable.

12 Interactive Systems

12.1 Interactive dialogue

Many systems allow individual users to interact with the computer directly. This involves the use of a dialogue between a terminal user and the computer. The most common basic types of interactive dialogue are:

        (a) menu selection
        (b) form filling
        (c) question and answer
        (d) interrogate or command.

In this chapter we develop program structures with allocated operations and conditions for each of the above. Each example is considered to be part of a larger problem - in practice it could be a self-contained procedure - and therefore we include only the structure, operations and conditions relevant to the dialogue.

When considering data structures for a screen dialogue one could argue that, so far as the program is concerned, the screen includes both input data, because user responses are 'accepted', and output data, because text is 'displayed'. However, all data on the screen, whether regarded as input or output, must appear sequentially, for example, prompt (output) then user response (input) and so on. Thus, there is no point in producing two separate structures and we shall develop just one data structure for each screen.

12.2 Menu selection

Consider the menu selection dialogue shown in figure 12.1.

The whole screen is used repeatedly until a user response of 'E' is received. If the user types anything other than A, D, I, R or E, an error message inviting him to try again is displayed at the bottom of the screen; the message is erased once the user has tried again. Valid responses invoke calls to separate procedures (one per option). A possible procedure for the ADD option is developed in the next section.

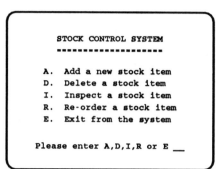

Figure 12.1

Thus the logical data structure consists of an iteration of screens, each of which is a sequence of the headings, followed by the menu, followed by the prompt, followed by the user response. Since the user must eventually type a valid response after having typed any number of invalid responses (including zero), we show an iteration of invalid response, followed by a valid response which is either A, D, I, R or E - see figure 12.2.

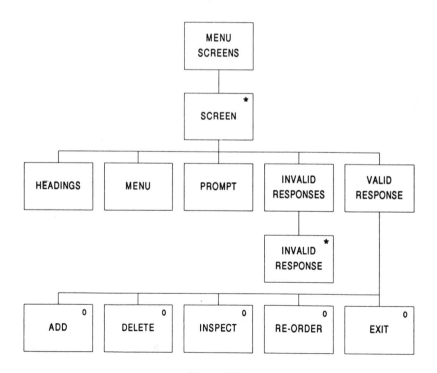

Figure 12.2

As there is only one data structure for this procedure, it will form the program structure and we can now produce a condition and operation list.

C1	Until user response = 'E'
C2	Until a valid response
C3	If user response = 'A'
C4	If user response = 'D'
C5	If user response = 'I'
C6	If user response = 'R'
1	Display headings on clear screen
2	Display menu lines
3	Display selection prompt
4	Accept user response
5	Display error message line (try again)
6	Clear error message line
7	Call 'Add' procedure
8	Call 'Delete' procedure
9	Call 'Inspect' procedure
10	Call 'Re-order' procedure
11	Initialise user response (to space)

The program structure is now given in figure 12.3 with allocated operations and conditions.

Examination of the program structure with allocated operations and conditions reveals a design consideration which will also appear in the next two examples. The condition C1 (until user response = 'E') cannot be implemented until the user has responded. We cannot employ the usual read ahead technique and allocate operation 4 (accept user response) to the beginning of MENU SCREENS, since it must come after the prompt. In effect we require the iteration MENU SCREENS BODY to have at least one occurrence of SCREEN. We can therefore overcome the problem in three ways.

The first way is by initialising the user response to a value other than 'E' at the beginning of MENU SCREENS. This is the approach adopted above, where operation 11 is included as an initialising operation to support the condition list.

The second way is to use QUIT from iteration. In this case, operation 11 and the component MENU SCREENS BODY would not have been included in figure 12.3. The condition C1 is omitted from the head of the iteration, and QUIT MENU SCREENS ITER is allocated to the component EXIT. We shall demonstrate this approach in section 12.4.

The third way is to implement the iteration in the target language as an iteration of at least one occurrence. For example, in the 'REPEAT statement(s) UNTIL condition' construct of Pascal, at least one occurrence of the

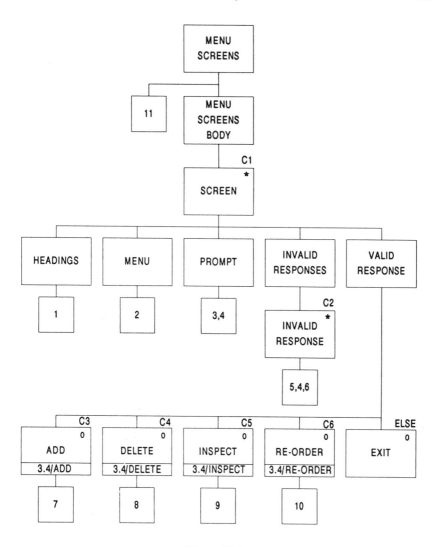

Figure 12.3

iteration is processed and the controlling condition is evaluated at the bottom of the loop. This can be implemented in COBOL by removing the code for 'if condition go to end of the iteration' from the start of the iteration and, at the end of the iteration, replacing the code for 'go to start of iteration' by the code for 'if not condition go to the start of the iteration'.

Having overcome the above problem, note that we can use a read ahead technique for the iteration INVALID RESPONSES. We allocate operation 4 as soon as the prompt has been displayed and once for every time the user must repeat to correct an error.

12.3 Form filling

A simple example of a form filling dialogue is now given in figure 12.4.

```
          STOCK CONTROL SYSTEM
          --------------------

             ADD NEW STOCK ITEM

        Stock number    _____
        Description        _____
        Location           _____
        Re-order level _____.__


    Confirm that the above is correct (Y/N) __
    Do you wish to repeat this transaction (Y/N) __
```

Figure 12.4

The whole of the 'form' is displayed on the screen and the terminal user is guided through it. The screen cursor is first positioned after 'stock number'; if the user enters an invalid stock number, an error message inviting him to try again is displayed at the bottom of the screen and the cursor returns to the appropriate position; the new stock number having been entered, the message disappears. After a valid response, the cursor moves to the description field position and so on. There is no validation for description, location or re-order level. After the four fields are completed, the user is asked if the information is correct; only if the response is affirmative are the data written to a direct access file. The user may then elect to repeat the transaction or not; if he wishes to do so, the entries on the form (but not the headings and skeleton) are cleared and the cursor returns to the stock number position. Also, for simplicity, we assume that Y or N (yes/no) responses are not validated (Y means yes, anything else means no).

The logical data structure is more complicated than for the menu selection - see figure 12.5. Note that stock number is shown as a sequence of an iteration of invalid entries (possibly zero) followed by a valid entry. This is because the user is forced to enter a valid stock number before continuing, after (possibly) entering a number of invalid ones.

Assuming that the record is written to a direct access file, we have no other data structures to take into account, the above data structure becomes the program structure and we can list the conditions and operations.

The program structure with allocated operations and conditions is now produced - see figure 12.6. You should examine it carefully. Note that the structure should be redrawn to include 'body' boxes after operations 9 and 10. Note also that we have exactly the same problem with C1 as we had in the previous example, and we overcome it in the same way.

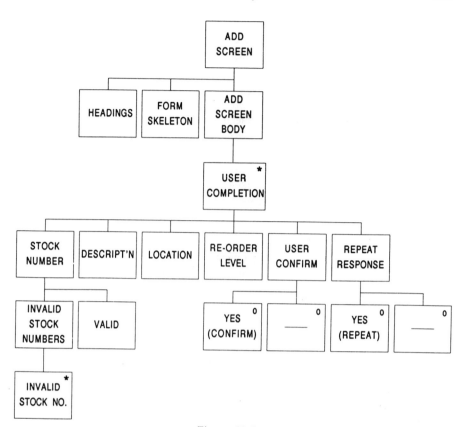

Figure 12.5

C1	Until user no longer wants to add new stock items (that is, until repeat response <> 'Y')
C2	Until stock number is a valid one
C3	If user confirmation = 'Y'
C4	If repeat response = 'Y'
1	Display headings on clear screen
2	Display form skeleton (that is, as in figure 12.4)
3	Accept stock number
4	Accept description
5	Accept location
6	Accept re-order level
7	Display error message line
8	Clear error message line
9	Accept confirm response
10	Accept repeat response
11	Clear form entries
12	Write new stock item record
13	Initialise repeat response (= 'Y')

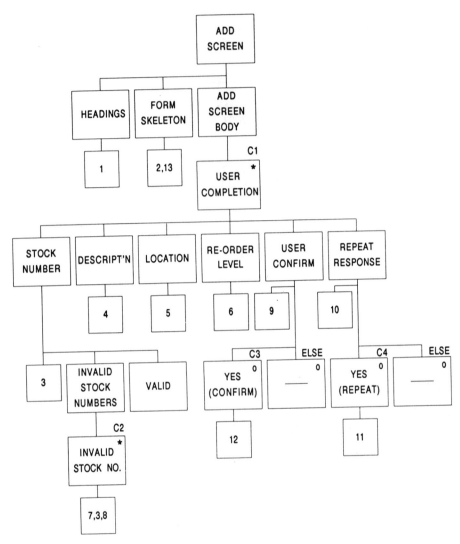

Figure 12.6

12.4 Question and answer

This type of dialogue, although normally not difficult to analyse, may often appear tedious when drawing data structures. We will consider a simple one by examining an example conversation which could be used to view the data of the previous example - see figure 12.7. The user input is shown in italics.

We can see that there are only 3 basic questions which lead to a number of responses by the user. The user's response determines what happens

```
WHAT STOCK NUMBER? 10004
ACCESS NOT ALLOWED
DO YOU WISH TO TRY AGAIN? y
WHAT STOCK NUMBER? 95006
DOES NOT EXIST
DO YOU WISH TO TRY AGAIN? y
WHAT STOCK NUMBER? 25632
O.K. WHAT FIELD? re-ord-level
DOES NOT EXIST
DO YOU WISH TO TRY AGAIN? y
WHAT STOCK NUMBER? 25632
O.K. WHAT FIELD? location
ACCESS NOT ALLOWED
DO YOU WISH TO TRY AGAIN? y
WHAT STOCK NUMBER? 26321
O.K. WHAT FIELD? description
O.K. BROWN LEATHER BOOTS SIZE 6
DO YOU WISH TO TRY AGAIN? n
EXIT
```

Figure 12.7

next. The response to 'WHAT STOCK NUMBER?' may be valid, with or without access rights, or invalid. If the number is valid (that is, if it exists) and the user has access rights, then he is asked to specify which field he wishes to view (O.K. WHAT FIELD?). Possible responses to this question are valid field names, with or without access rights, or an invalid field name. Entering a valid field name with access rights produces the appropriate data value (O.K. BROWN LEATHER BOOTS SIZE 6). Whenever an invalid stock number or invalid field is entered, the same message (DOES NOT EXIST) is displayed; similarly, whenever access is not allowed, the same message (ACCESS NOT ALLOWED) is displayed. Once either of these messages or the appropriate data has been displayed, the user is invited to re-try (DO YOU WISH TO TRY AGAIN?). A response of 'y' leads to a repeat of the above, beginning with 'WHAT STOCK NUMBER?', otherwise the dialogue terminates with EXIT.

We can use the sample dialogue to identify the order and grouping of the data, before drawing the data structure. At the top level we recognise that the dialogue is a sequence of Q & A DIALOGUE BODY followed by EXIT. The body of the dialogue is then an iteration of USER REQUEST, which consists of the lines from 'WHAT STOCK NUMBER?' to 'DO YOU WISH TO TRY AGAIN?'. USER REQUEST is a sequence of the what stock number question, followed by the lines dealing with a specific stock number, followed by the try again question. Now, by incorporating the appropriate selections, we arrive at the data structure shown in figure 12.8.

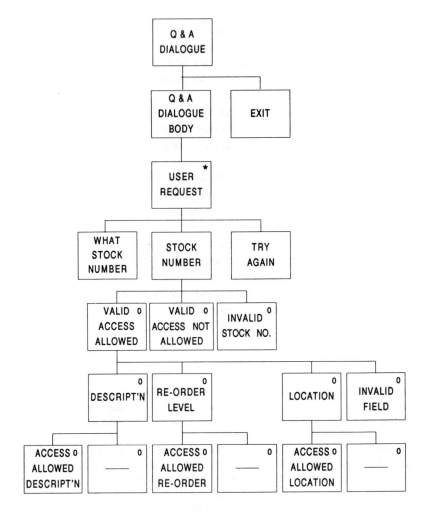

Figure 12.8

This type of deeply nested selection dominated structure can often be simplified by employing the POSIT/ADMIT construct. We could, for each stock number, presume (or POSIT) a valid request with access rights resulting in the appropriate data being displayed, unless forced to admit this is not true. When the admit path (that is, not valid or no access rights) is taken we have a simple choice of two different error messages.

The simplified structure is shown in figure 12.9.

If we assume direct access to the required information, then figure 12.9 is the only logical data structure which will influence our design. We can, therefore, proceed with the condition list and operation list.

Once again the condition C1 is difficult to implement until the user has had an opportunity to respond to the 'try again' question. It should be

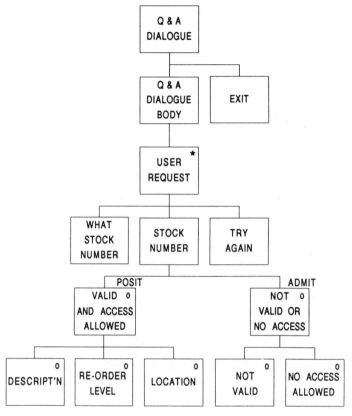

Figure 12.9

C1	Until user response (try again) <> 'Y'
C2	If field = DESCRIPTION
C3	If field = RE-ORDER LEVEL
C4	If stock number or field invalid
1	Display 'what stock number' prompt
2	Accept user response (stock number)
3	Display 'try again' prompt
4	Accept user response (try again)
5	Display 'does not exist'
6	Display 'what field' prompt
7	Accept user response (field)
8	Attempt to retrieve required stock item
9	Display description
10	Display re-order level
11	Display location
12	Display 'exit'
13	Display 'access not allowed'

noted that by including the question right at the beginning of the dialogue as well, we would remove the difficulty as we could then use the standard read ahead technique. Nevertheless, in this example, we demonstrate how QUIT from iteration can overcome the problem. The allocation of the conditions and operations to the program structure is fairly easy, so for demonstration purposes only, we will go straight to the schematic logic - see figure 12.10. You should examine it carefully, paying particular attention to the QUITs from POSIT and the QUIT from iteration. You will notice that, in this case, the QUIT from iteration has an associated condition.

```
Q+A DIALOGUE SEQ
  Q+A DIALOGUE BODY ITER (no condition defined at the top)
    USER REQUEST SEQ
      WHAT STOCK NUMBER
        DO 1 [Display 'what stock number' prompt
        DO 2 [Accept user response (stock number)
      WHAT STOCK NUMBER END
      STOCK NUMBER POSIT valid and allowable request
        VALID AND ACCESS ALLOWED SEQ
          DO 8 [Attempt to retrieve required stock item
          QUIT STOCK NUMBER POSIT IF C5 [no stock item retrieved
          QUIT STOCK NUMBER POSIT IF C6 [no access rights for
                                                   stock item
          DO 6 [Display 'what field' prompt
          DO 7 [Accept user response (field)
          QUIT STOCK NUMBER POSIT IF C7 [field name invalid
          VALID AND ACCESS ALLOWED BODY SEL IF C2 [field =
                                                   DESCRIPTION
            DESCRIPTION
              QUIT STOCK NUMBER POSIT IF C8 [no access rights
                                                 for descript.
              DO 9 [Display description
            DESCRIPTION END
          VALID AND ACCESS ALLOWED BODY ELSE 1 IF C3 [field =
                                                   RE-ORDER
            RE-ORDER LEVEL
              QUIT STOCK NUMBER POSIT IF C9 [no access rights
                                                 for re-order
              DO 10 [Display re-order level
            RE-ORDER LEVEL END
          VALID AND ACCESS ALLOWED BODY ELSE 2
            LOCATION
              QUIT STOCK NUMBER POSIT IF C10 [no access rights
                                                 for location
              DO 11 [Display location
            LOCATION END
          VALID AND ACCESS ALLOWED BODY END
        VALID AND ACCESS ALLOWED END
      STOCK NUMBER ADMIT request is not (valid and allowable)
```

Figure 12.10 (above and on following page)

```
     NOT VALID OR NO ACCESS SEL IF C4 [stock number or field
                                              invalid
        NOT VALID
          DO 5 [Display 'does not exist'
        NOT VALID END
     NOT VALID OR NO ACCESS ELSE 1
        NO ACCESS ALLOWED
          DO 13 [Display 'access not allowed'
        NO ACCESS ALLOWED END
     NOT VALID OR NO ACCESS END
   STOCK NUMBER END
   TRY AGAIN
     DO 3 [Display try again prompt
     DO 4 [Accept user response (try again)
     QUIT Q+A DIALOGUE BODY ITER IF C1 [again response <> 'Y'
   TRY AGAIN END
 USER REQUEST END
Q+A DIALOGUE BODY END
EXIT
 DO 12 [Display 'exit'
EXIT END
Q+A DIALOGUE END
```

12.5 Interrogate or command

Consider a direct access file containing student names with their project title. A simple command language to interrogate this file might consist of three commands: FIND, PRINT and EXIT. The formats could be:

(a) FIND attribute = value
(b) PRINT attribute
(c) EXIT
   where attribute may be NAME or TITLE

An example of the dialogue with computer responses in *italics* is shown in figure 12.11.

A data structure to reflect this dialogue is quite simple. We obviously have an iteration of command until the user types 'EXIT'. There are two other valid commands, so we need to indicate the choice. Then for both FIND and PRINT there is a choice of attributes. An attribute value (in the FIND command) may be found or not found. The data structure, which is essentially driven by the possible user inputs, is shown in figure 12.12.

We will assume that the direct access file has no extra influence on our design; figure 12.12 becomes the program structure.

```
FIND NAME = SMITH
not found
FIND NAME = BROWN
found
PRINT TOTLE
no such attribute
PRINT TITLE
Graphics in Ada
FIND TOTLE = RELATIONAL DATABASE
no such attribute
FIND TITLE = RELATIONAL DATABASE
found
PRING NAME
no such command
PRINT NAME
P.Forster
EXIT
```

Figure 12.11

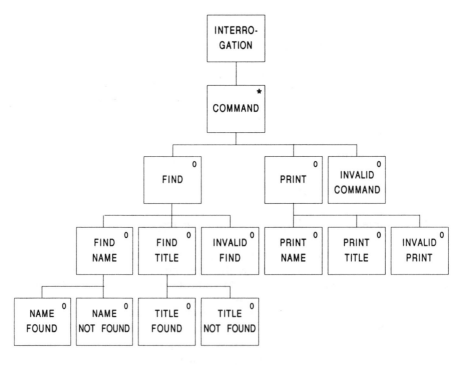

Figure 12.12

The revised program structure with allocated operations and conditions (below) is given in figure 12.13.

C1	Until user command EXIT
C2	If command = FIND
C3	If command = PRINT
C4	If attribute = NAME
C5	If attribute = TITLE
C6	If required name found
C7	If required title found
1	Accept command string
2	Get symbol (command)
3	Get symbol (attribute)
4	Get symbol (value)
5	Attempt to retrieve record with required name
6	Attempt to retrieve record with required title
7	Display name
8	Display title
9	Display 'not found'
10	Display 'found'
11	Display 'no such command'
12	Display 'no such attribute'
13	Initialise name and title to null

Note that operations 2 to 4 may well be implemented as a single parameterised subprogram which delivers the required character string. Operation 13 is used so that there is no need to insist on a valid FIND before a PRINT.

12.6 Exercises

12.6.1 Design an interactive procedure which allows the terminal user to choose between capturing details of persons' home addresses or details of their family cars. Use a simple menu selection dialogue for the choice, similar to that described in section 12.2, and form filling dialogues for the data capture functions, similar to that described in section 12.3.

Each address has three lines, name, road and town, and the car details form should capture the person's name, car make and model. There is no validation on either form.

You may assume that all data are written to a direct access file.

You should use separate subprograms for the menu selection, the address data capture and the car details capture.

Continue your design as far as the production of program structures with allocated operations and conditions. For each screen, briefly explain how you would use QUIT out of iteration to overcome the 'read ahead' difficulty discussed in section 12.2.

12.6.2 Design an interactive procedure to view the car detail records of the previous exercise by means of a dialogue typified by that shown in figure 12.14. The user input is shown in italics.

```
WHICH PERSON? A M Smith
DOES NOT EXIST
DO YOU WISH TO TRY ANOTHER NAME? y
WHICH PERSON? N Zaini
O.K. WHICH FIELD? type
DOES NOT EXIST
DO YOU WISH TO TRY ANOTHER FIELD? y
O.K. WHICH FIELD? make
O.K. FORD
DO YOU WISH TO TRY ANOTHER FIELD? y
O.K. WHICH FIELD? model
O.K. SIERRA
DO YOU WISH TO TRY ANOTHER FIELD? n
DO YOU WISH TO TRY ANOTHER NAME? y
WHICH PERSON? G A Roberts
DOES NOT EXIST
DO YOU WISH TO TRY ANOTHER NAME? n
EXIT
```

Figure 12.14

You may assume that all features of the dialogue have been included here and that data are held in a direct access file in records containing name, car make and car model.

Continue your design as far as the production of a program structure with allocated operations and conditions. In this case do not use backtracking or quit out of iteration.

If you wish, you may now attempt the case study in appendix E.

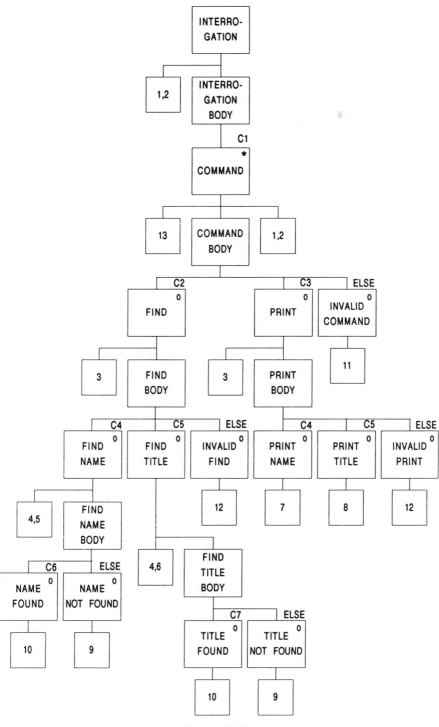

Figure 12.13

13 Testing, Documentation and Program Amendment

13.1 Testing

13.1.1 What to test

By now you should appreciate that the main feature of JSP is the way in which we proceed from data structures to program code, through well-defined manageable stages (please refer to section 1.4.). You should also have realised that if we make a mistake, then certain errors may become apparent at an early stage. For example, if data structures without clashes cannot be combined easily, then the structures should be carefully checked to see if they are correct. If you cannot find an obvious position on the program structure for a certain operation, then you should first ascertain whether or not that operation is necessary and then, provided it is, check the program structure. Having taken due care in applying the principles and rules of JSP, you should always be reasonably confident that the program is correct.

However, mistakes can still occur and obviously further testing should be incorporated, in keeping with the philosophy of 'identifying errors as soon as possible'. We can test the design once the program structure with allocated operations and conditions has been produced and when we have produced the final schematic logic. In each case, we check the structure, overall logic and data values - in particular, the results to be output. Such details as the correct formats for input and correct layout for output are not included in the elementary operations and therefore cannot be checked until later. They have to be checked at a later stage when testing the program code.

In addition, we may need to test for compatibility with associated software, which means ensuring that programs or subprograms interact correctly. We may also need to test for customer (or user) satisfaction (often called acceptance trials).

13.1.2 Testing the design

We shall describe a method of testing the design by means of a so-called desk check (trace table or dry run) using the program structure with allocated conditions and operations. The principles described apply also to testing the design using the schematic logic.

For example, consider the sales report program (figure 5.3 in chapter 5). Given the program structure with allocated operations and conditions, we must first devise some test data. This aspect of testing will be considered in more detail in section 13.2; here, for illustrative purposes we shall use the following:

```
            AREA  YEAR  PRODUCT  SALES VALUE
1st record   A    92    PENS        300
2nd record   B    92    PENCILS     500
3rd record   B    93    RUBBERS      50
            end of file indicator
```

We then record the results that should be achieved, remembering that, at this stage, we cannot check the precise layout:

Headings for area A
Sales 100 to 300 line for 300 pens
Year total (for '92) of 300
Area total (for A) of 300
Headings for area B
Sales over 300 line for 500 pencils
Year total (for '92) of 500
Sales under 100 line for 50 rubbers
Year total (for '93) of 50
Area total (for B) of 550

Next we head up a sheet of paper with the names of data areas to be used in the program. One way of doing this for the sales report problem is illustrated in figure 13.1. Then we process the test data by hand, doing only what is indicated by the program structure. Changes to data area contents and the values of conditional expressions are noted. For each output operation we check the current value(s) in the table against the results that should be achieved, for example, the first occurrence of operation 5 should output headings for area A. The start of the trace table is shown in figure 13.1.

We will not complete the desk check here, but invite you to do so. As the test data leads us to the operations and conditions (including the ELSE) they should be ticked off on the program structure.

Finally, when we have exhausted the test data, we check that:

1. We have achieved the correct results.
2. We have ticked off every operation and condition on the program structure. If we have not, we need more exhaustive test data and should repeat the process.

Testing the design will ensure that we have the correct structure, and have correctly allocated operations and conditions. Also it may reveal possible coding pitfalls. For instance, suppose that the appropriate area was to be included in the area total line. As we arrive at operation 6 in the dry run, we would read off a correct value of 300 for area total, a value of B for area and A for stored area. We would then note that stored area (and not area from the current record) should be used when coding operation 6.

OPERATIONS/ CONDITIONS	CURRENT SALES RECORD				STORED AREA	STORED YEAR	AREA TOTAL	YEAR TOTAL	OUTPUT
	AREA	YEAR	PRODUCT	VALUE					
1									
4	A	92	PENS	300					
C1 (false)									
5									✓
13							0		
15					A				
C2 (false)									
14								0	
16						92			
C3 (false)									
C4 (false)									
C5 (true)									
9									✓
11							300		
12								300	
4	B	92	PENCILS	500					
C3 (true)									
7									✓
C2 (true)									
6									✓

Figure 13.1

13.1.3 Testing the coding

We must test the program code to ensure that the elementary operations, conditions and control constructs of the program structure and schematic logic are correctly translated into the target language (see chapter 7). This includes checking the precise details of input and output layouts against the problem specification.

The principles that we have seen in testing the design obviously apply to testing the coding. We must obtain suitable test data; we must know what results are correct and we must aim to test as thoroughly as possible.

Testing the coding will obviously involve using the computer and, as such, the programmer might be able to utilise testing software such as trace programs and debugging aids. These vary considerably from computer to computer so we will not attempt a description here. Rather, we will give a list of the objectives to be met in this aspect of program testing.

1. Ensure that each program statement is executed at least once. This is an obvious point, although it is sometimes not achieved, particularly in the handling of rare error conditions.
2. Ensure that each type of input data has been read at least once. In particular, with variable length fields and records, minimum and maximum lengths should have been specified.
3. Ensure that each type of output data has been written at least once. For example, in printed output check detail lines, headings, total lines, footings etc.
4. Ensure that the terminating condition for each iteration is used. Take care to allow for the alternatives in compound conditions.
5. Ensure that each selection condition is used. Do not forget the ELSE.
6. Ensure that each program statement gives the expected result. Beware of data truncation, rounding, accuracy etc.

13.2 Producing test data using STM

13.2.1 What is STM?

Although there are some aids to the production of test data, this task is still viewed as a chore by many programmers, with the result that test data choice is often poor. It is not sufficient merely to test according to simple criteria, such as, there are four record types so we need four records in the test data. So-called 'white-box' testing methods use the internal states of the program, as revealed by the program structure, to direct the testing. Paths through the program are identified, then test data are produced to exercise these paths. The objective is to maximise the possibility of discovering program errors, but using the minimum number of test data cases.

The Structural Testing Method (STM)[#] has been specifically developed to test JSP designed programs. Paths through the program structure are described in terms of sequences of program conditions and referred to as condition paths.

[#] M. Roper and P. Smith, 'A Structural Testing Method for JSP Designed Programs', *Software - Practice and Experience*, Vol. 17(2), 135-137 (1987).

The method has three stages:

1. The derivation of a 'conditional expression' from a pre-order traversal of the program structure. This is a single 'conditional expression', consisting of program conditions and conditional operators.
2. The use of the STM algebra to expand the 'conditional expression', in order to find all 'condition paths' through the program.
3. The production of test data cases and combining 'condition paths', as applicable, to minimise the number of test runs.

Since the algebraic notation is used when producing the conditional expression, we shall first explain the STM algebra, then describe how to produce the conditional expression before applying the complete method to a specific example.

13.2.2 The STM algebra

The STM algebra is similar to ordinary boolean algebra. It can be described in terms of the following operators:

$\overline{A}$	means	NOT A
$A \cap B$	means	A AND B
$A \cup B$	means	A OR B
AB	means	A then B (one condition then another as a sequence)

The letters A and B represent simple conditions (that is, non-compound relational expressions). For example,

the program condition	'not (deduction code 20 and amount > £1)'
would be expressed as	$\overline{C1 \cap C2}$
where	C1 is 'deduction code 20'
	C2 is 'amount > £1'.

Similarly,

the program condition	'end of file or change of area'
would be expressed as	$C3 \cup C4$
where	C3 is 'end of file'
	C4 is 'change of area'.

In order to simplify boolean expressions we make use of De Morgan's Laws. These are:

(1) $\overline{A \cap B}$ is equivalent to $\overline{A} \cup \overline{B}$

(2) $\overline{C \cup D}$ is equivalent to $\overline{C} \cap \overline{D}$

We shall now illustrate the first rule. Suppose the variable x can only have the values 1, 2, 3, 4, 5, 6, 7, 8, then

A	x>2	is true for the values 3, 4, 5, 6, 7, 8
B	x<6	is true for the values 1, 2, 3, 4, 5
A∩B		is true for the values 3, 4, 5
$\overline{A∩B}$		is true for the values 1, 2, 6, 7, 8

and

$\overline{A}$	x<=2	is true for the values 1, 2
$\overline{B}$	x>=6	is true for the values 6, 7, 8
$\overline{A∪B}$		is true for the values 1, 2, 6, 7, 8

You might like to use a similar approach to illustrate the second rule.

In STM, we derive a conditional expression from the program structure and then expand it according to the following rules:

(1) AB gives   A,B (the path taken when A is true, then B is true).

(2) A∪B gives   A (this describes one path)
                 B (this describes another path)

Note that (1) has a higher precedence than (2). For example,

(a) AB ∪ $\overline{A}$ gives $\overline{A}$ (path 1)
                                         A,B   (path 2)

(b) (A∩B)(C∪D)   gives   A∩B, C   (path 1)
                             A∩B, D   (path 2)

(c) (A∩B)C ∪ D   gives   A∩B, C   (path 1)
                             D   (path 2)

(d) $\overline{C1}$ $\overline{(C2∩C3)}$ C1 ∪ C1   gives $\overline{C1}$ $\overline{(C2∪C3)}$ C1 ∪ C1 (De Morgan)
                    that is $\overline{C1}$ _____(path 1)
                    and $\overline{C1}$ $\overline{(C2∪C3)}$ C1
         which becomes $\overline{C1}$, $\overline{C2}$, C1 (path 2)
                         $\overline{C1}$, $\overline{C3}$, C1 (path 3)

If necessary, expressions can be expanded in stages, as in (d) above. Note that the conditions are in the order in which they are encountered along the path and thus do not have to be true simultaneously. This means that A $\overline{A}$ is meaningful, A is true at the first evaluation, NOT A is true at the next one.

13.2.3 Deriving conditional expressions

The conditional expression is a single expression, written in terms of program conditions, which describes all of the condition paths through the program. Before tackling a complete program, we shall state the conditional expression and examine the directed graph of condition paths for each of the basic JSP constructs. The directed graph helps us to visualise the condition paths. The beginning and end of non-elementary components are indicated by 'b' and 'e' respectively.

(a) Sequence - see figure 13.2

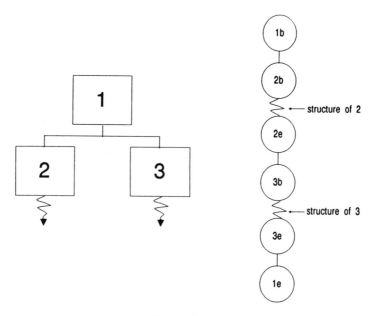

Figure 13.2

A sequence does not involve any conditions and therefore only one path exists. For figure 13.2, the conditional expression (expr.1) is:

    expr.1 :   (expr.2)(expr.3)

(b) Selection - see figure 13.3

Each selection component with a simple (that is, non-compound) condition generates one path. Notice that the ELSE, which normally governs the final choice, has to be replaced by the appropriate specific condition. In this case, because we have only two choices, the ELSE becomes $\overline{C1}$.

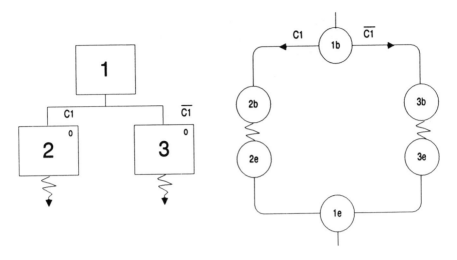

Figure 13.3

For figure 13.3 the conditional expression (expr.1) is:

expr.1 : $C1(\text{expr.2}) \cup \overline{C1}(\text{expr.3})$

(c) *Iteration with simple condition and at least one occurrence of the iteration component part - see figure 13.4*

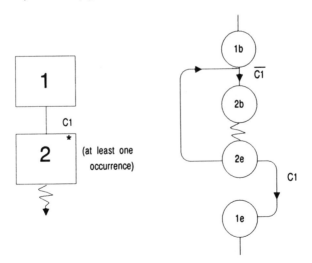

Figure 13.4

When the iteration component part is executed at least once, we have a conditional expression of the form: the condition $(\overline{C1})$ which causes the iteration component part (2 in figure 13.4) to be executed, the expression for the component part, and the terminating condition (C1). This gives the conditional expression (expr.1) for figure 13.4:

expr.1 : $\overline{C1}$ (expr.2) C1

(d) *Iteration with simple condition and zero or more occurrences of the iteration component - see figure 13.5*

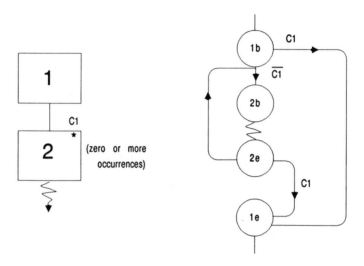

Figure 13.5

The possibility of zero iterations introduces another path. The conditional expression (expr.1) for figure 13.5 is:

expr.1 : $\overline{C1}$ (expr.2) C1 ∪ C1

(e) *Iteration with a compound condition - see figure 13.6*

Using figure 13.6, and assuming that we must execute the iteration component part at least once, we produce an initial expression as in part (c) above:

expr.1 : $\overline{(C1 \cup C2)}$ (C1 ∪ C2)
   or   : $(\overline{C1} \cap \overline{C2})$ (C1 ∪ C2)   (using De Morgan's law)

giving the expressions:

$(\overline{C1} \cap \overline{C2})$ C1
$(\overline{C1} \cap \overline{C2})$ C2

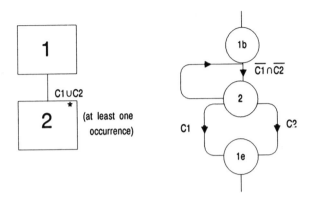

Figure 13.6

which identify the two terminating conditions (C1 and C2).

Note that an elementary component (for example, 2 in figure 13.6) does not generate a sub-expression (expr.N).

The example shown in figure 13.6 illustrates the difference between a 'route' through a program and a 'condition path'. For example, the route through the program would be: the beginning of component 1, then component 2, then the end of component 1; the latter part of this route however, may be achieved by either of the condition paths C1 or C2.

13.2.4 Applying the method

Consider a program to produce a simple sales analysis. Each record of the input file contains region code, salesman's name and sales-figure. The file is sorted in ascending order of region code. The required output is a report that lists the details of each salesman and, at the end of each region, the number of salesmen who have achieved a sales target in excess of 100 units. The program structure with allocated conditions is shown in figure 13.7 and the directed graph is shown as figure 13.8. The condition list is:

C1	End of file
C2	Different region
C3	Sales > 100 units

The outer iteration is classified as 'zero or more' to allow for an empty input file (in which case the inner iteration will never be reached). For a non-empty file, the inner iteration will be reached and there will then be at least one occurrence of SALES RECORD.

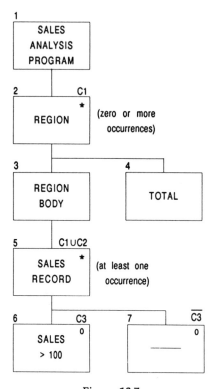

Figure 13.7

Notice how we have implemented other conventions specific to STM: components are numbered; the use of simple (that is, non-compound) conditions; and $\overline{C3}$ replacing ELSE.

We now write down the conditional expression (using the component numbers as identifiers) for each component, ignoring the elementary ones.

expr.1	:	$\overline{C1}$ (expr.2) C1 ∪ C1	[see (d) in section 13.2.3]
expr.2	:	expr.3	[see (a) in section 13.2.3]
expr.3	:	$(\overline{C1 \cup C2})$ (expr.5) (C1 ∪ C2)	[see (e) in section 13.2.3]
expr.5	:	C3 ∪ $\overline{C3}$	[see (b) in section 13.2.3]

Now, starting at the bottom, we substitute the conditional expressions one at a time into an expression above it until we have a single expression for expr.1.

expr.3	:	$(\overline{C1 \cup C2})$ (C3 ∪ $\overline{C3}$) (C1 ∪ C2)
expr.2	:	$(\overline{C1 \cup C2})$ (C3 ∪ $\overline{C3}$) (C1 ∪ C2)
expr.1	:	$\overline{C1}$ $(\overline{C1 \cup C2})$ (C3 ∪ $\overline{C3}$) (C1 ∪ C2) C1 ∪ C1

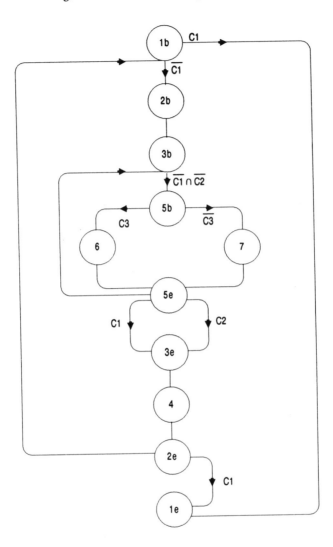

Figure 13.8

We apply De Morgan's laws as necessary for compound conditions. In our case, we arrive at:

expr.1 : $\overline{C1}\ (\overline{C1} \cap \overline{C2})\ (C3 \cup \overline{C3})\ (C1 \cup C2)\ C1\ \cup\ C1$

Now we separate the expression into individual condition paths. Essentially, we look for ORs and divide the conditional expression at these points remembering that ORs have a lower precedence than condition sequences.

This gives us the following paths:

path 1	$\overline{C1}$, $\overline{C1} \cap \overline{C2}$, C3, C1, C1
path 2	$\overline{C1}$, $\overline{C1} \cap \overline{C2}$, $\overline{C3}$, C1, C1
path 3	$\overline{C1}$, $\overline{C1} \cap \overline{C2}$, C3, C2, C1
path 4	$\overline{C1}$, $\overline{C1} \cap \overline{C2}$, $\overline{C3}$, C2, C1
path 5	C1

We need to examine the specification of the program to determine the layout and contents of the test data records. In our example, we have a simple record layout containing region code, name and sales.

Now we look at each condition path in turn and produce appropriate test data. In our example, we get:

path 1	Region A	W. ANDREW	101
	end of file		
path 2	Region A	F. STEVENS	86
	end of file		
path 3	Region A	R. GREENFIELD	199
	Region B	D. GRAY	156
	end of file		
path 4	Region A	P. WRIGHT	99
	Region B	R. SMIT	20
	end of file		
path 5	end of file		

We arrived at this data for each path by examining each condition in turn, and deducing the corresponding requirements in terms of actual data. We can use path 4 to illustrate this.

$\overline{C1}$	not end of file	- at least one record
$\overline{C1} \cap \overline{C2}$	not end of file and	
	not different region	- no additional requirement
$\overline{C3}$	not (sales > 100 units)	- sales <= 100 (that is, 99)
C2	different region	- another record with a different region
C1	end of file	- no more data

Thus, the critical aspects of the data given for this path are: the sales value of 99, a change of region from A to B, and the end of file.

By examining the condition paths, we may be able to combine some paths and hence reduce the number of test data cases. For example, in path

3, having changed the region to leave the inner iteration, we must re-enter it to process the second record and detect end of file. This suggests that the sequence of conditions C3, C1 from path 1 could be exercised after the C3, C2 in path 3. These two paths can therefore be combined to give:

path 1&3 $\overline{C1}$, $\overline{C1} \cap \overline{C2}$, C3, C2, C3, C1, C1

with corresponding test data:

path 1&3	Region A	R. GREENFIELD	199
	Region B	D. GRAY	156
	end of file		

Paths 2 and 4 could be combined in a similar manner. Although combining paths in this way may reduce the number of test runs, there are inherent problems. It may not be feasible, it is largely intuitive, and care must be taken to ensure that all the original paths are retained.

13.3 Documentation

Documentation should proceed throughout the design process. JSP certainly yields useful documentation at each of the design stages. In this text we have indicated the general way in which structure diagrams and schematic logic could be presented. Specific standards will exist in most computer installations in respect of cross-referencing, size and format. In fact, although attempts are made to provide widely accepted standards of documentation, there is a wide variety of opinion as to what is required and the format of documents.

The principle to guide us is:

> The documentation should enable someone other than the originator, but who is familiar with the design methods and documentation standards, to fully understand the program's purpose and the way that purpose has been achieved.

To this end one might consider producing a documentation file for a computer program from the following list:

1. The specification including record, screen and print layouts.
2. Data structures.
3. Revised program structure(s) with allocated operations and conditions.
4. Operation and condition lists.
5. Schematic logic(s) (unoptimised).

6. Revised schematic logic(s) when backtracking is used.
7. Optimised schematic logic(s).
8. The source code with suitable comments to describe each component.
9. A test plan with annotated test results.
10. Amendments list.

13.4 Program amendment

It is a fact of life that all applications programs will need amending or enhancing during their lifetime. Indeed, many programming departments spend a majority of their resources in program maintenance.

Often programmers do not like the program maintenance task because it may be tedious and frustrating due to a lack of adequate documentation or sloppy programming practice. If a program has been designed according to a reasonable design method, then the maintenance should be that much easier and satisfying.

From what we have seen of JSP, it should be apparent that amendments (enhancements) are of two basic types:

(a) functional
(b) structural.

We must first be able to make this distinction. Never be tempted to attempt coding modifications without first assessing the scale and type of the amendment and making the changes necessary at each design stage.

A functional amendment is one that merely affects the elementary operations (or conditions). We might ask ourselves:

"Can I change one (or more) of the existing operations?"
or "Can I simply add one (or more) operations?"

If we answer 'yes' to either of the above, we can test our answer by (re)allocating the operation(s) to the program structure. If this task is in any way difficult, then we should investigate further to see if the amendment is structural.

For a structural amendment, a change is made to one or more of the data structures. In such a case one proceeds through each stage of the design making all necessary changes at each stage.

It is obvious that the distinction between the two types of amendment is crucial to planning the work of a department. The former will generally take a very short time, the latter considerably longer.

We defined the main requirements of a software design method (see section 1.2 in chapter 1) as enabling correct programs to be produced and facilitating the organised control of software projects. Most software projects will involve a high proportion of maintenance as user requirements change. Using JSP will help the production of correct software and ensure that it remains correct during its lifetime of inevitable amendment.

13.5 Exercises

13.5.1 Test the design of the program produced for exercise 4.3.2 (see solution for exercise 5.4.2), by first stating the expected results and then producing a trace table, using the following data:

	Ward	Name	Patient or Staff
record 1	A100	J G SMITH	PATIENT
record 2	A100	J L THOMAS	PATIENT
record 3	A100	B C WHITE	STAFF
record 4	B300	A B GREEN	STAFF
	end of file indicator		

13.5.2 Test the design of the collate problem from chapter 8 in which only those keys present on one or both of the input files are processed (see figure 8.6 and associated operation and condition lists).

Using the following data (9999 acts as an end of file indicator), state the expected results and then produce a trace table.

FILE A (key value)	FILE B (key value)
1235	1468
1468	1532
1532	9999
9999	

Are the data sufficient?

13.5.3 Expand the following conditional expressions using STM algebra:

(a) C1 (C2∩C3) $\overline{C1}$ ∪ $\overline{C1}$

(b) C1 (C2∩C1) (C3∪C4) $\overline{C1}$ ∪ (C5∪C6)

(c) C1 (C2∪C3) $(\overline{C4∪C5})$

(d) C1 $(\overline{C2∩C3})$ (C7∩C8) (C4∪C5) $\overline{C1}$ ∪ $\overline{C1}$

(e) C1 (C5∪C6) $(\overline{C3∩C4})$ $\overline{C1}$ ∪ $\overline{C1}$

13.5.4 For exercise 4.3.1 (see also solution 4.3.1 in appendix A)

  (a) Draw the program structure with allocated conditions using STM conventions.
  (b) Draw the directed graph of condition paths.
  (c) Derive the conditional expression.
  (d) Expand the conditional expression to obtain all condition paths.
  (e) Produce appropriate test data cases. (Each record in the input file contains a machine description and a 'due for repacement' indicator.)

13.5.5 For exercise 4.3.2 (see also solution 4.3.2 in appendix A)

  (a) Draw the program structure with allocated conditions using STM conventions.
  (b) Draw the directed graph of condition paths.
  (c) Derive the conditional expression.
  (d) Expand the conditional expression to obtain all condition paths.
  (e) Produce appropriate test data cases. (Each record in the input file contains a ward code, a name, and a 'staff/patient' indicator.)

Appendix A : Solutions to Exercises

The specimen solutions given in this appendix may have equally correct alternatives. In particular, the annotated sketches contain the minimum amount of data to illustrate the groupings, in most cases showing the boundaries of the various groups only.

Chapter 2

2.4.1

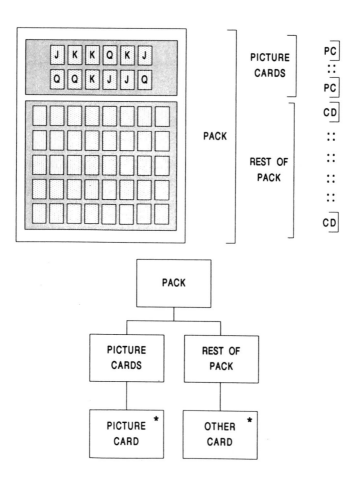

2.4.2

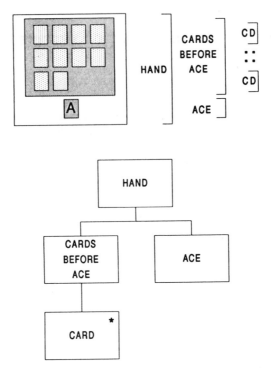

CARDS BEFORE ACE is an iteration of CARD. An iteration may be of zero occurrences, so the minimum number of cards in the hand is one - an ace.

2.4.3

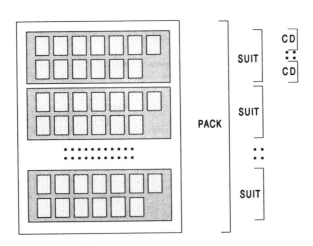

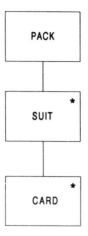

2.4.4

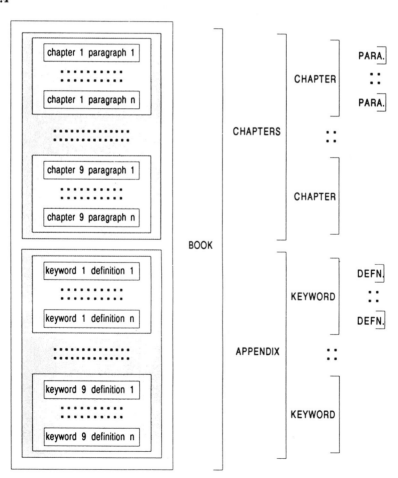

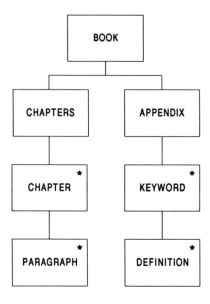

2.4.5

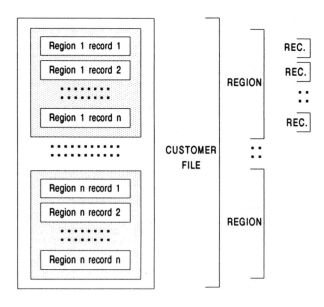

2.4.6

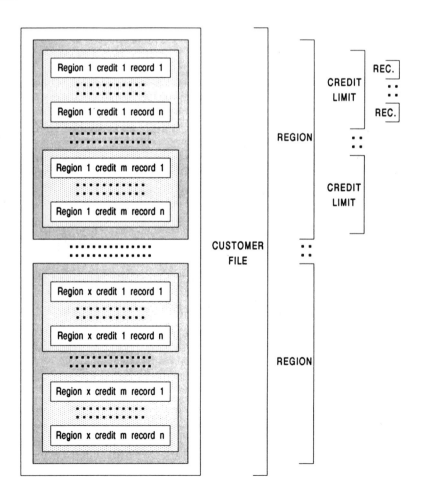

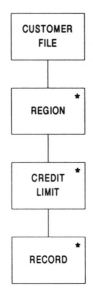

2.4.7

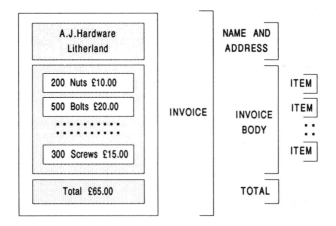

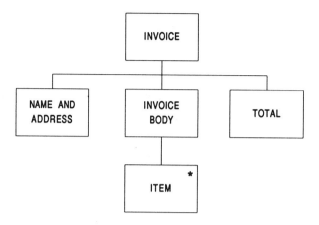

2.4.8

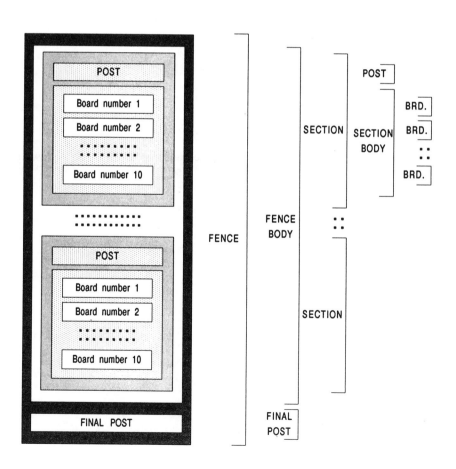

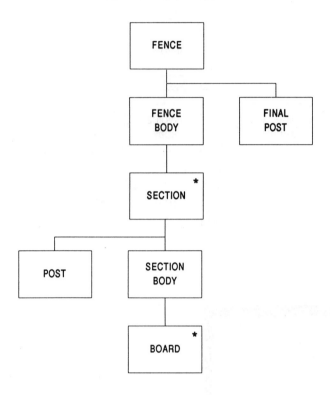

Alternatively, we could regard FENCE as a sequence of FIRST POST followed by FENCE BODY. SECTION would then be a sequence of SECTION BODY followed by POST.

2.4.9

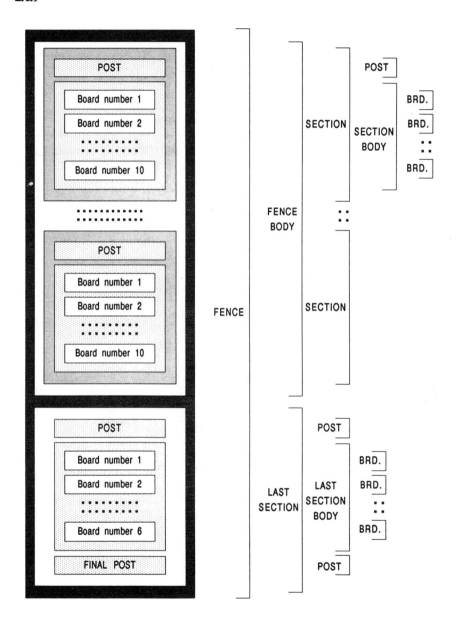

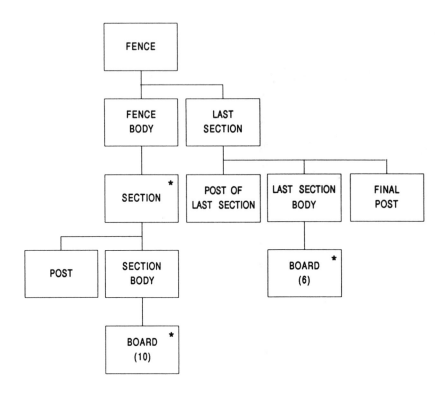

2.4.10

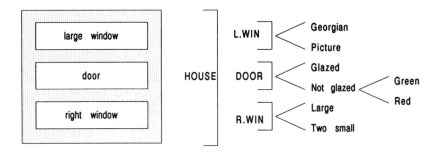

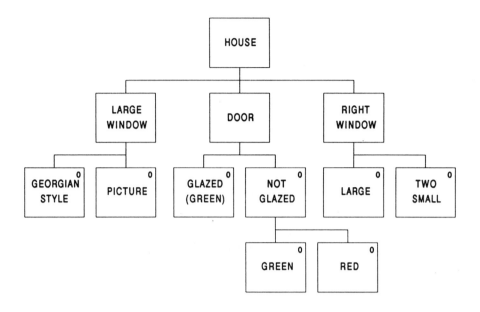

2.4.11

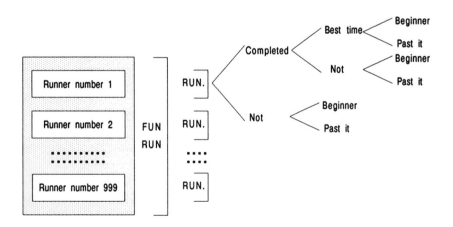

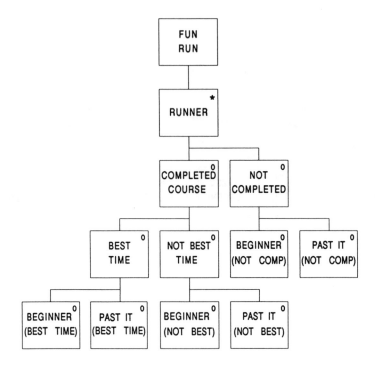

There are a number of possible solutions to this problem because we do not know which of the various selections should be at the top level. More knowledge of the problem that we are trying to solve and the physical order of the data would enable us to decide upon the most appropriate structure.

2.4.12

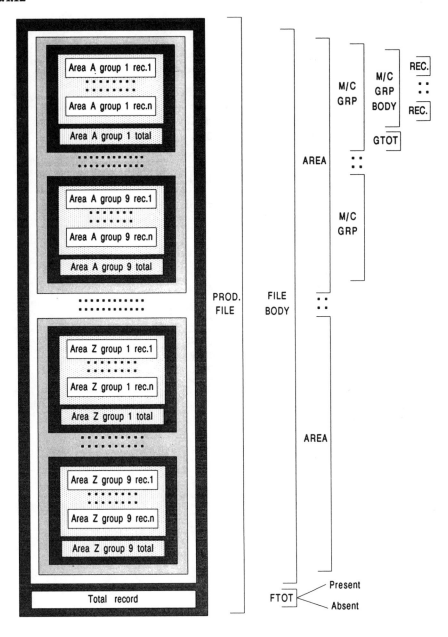

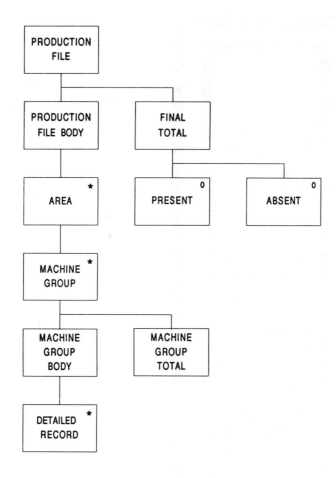

Chapter 3

3.3.1

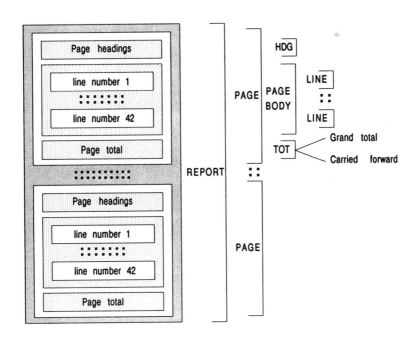

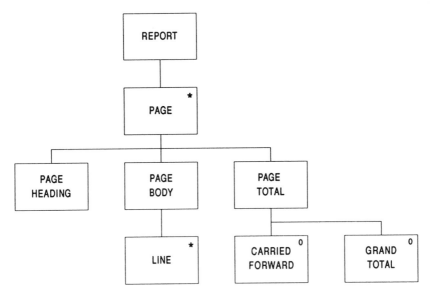

3.3.2

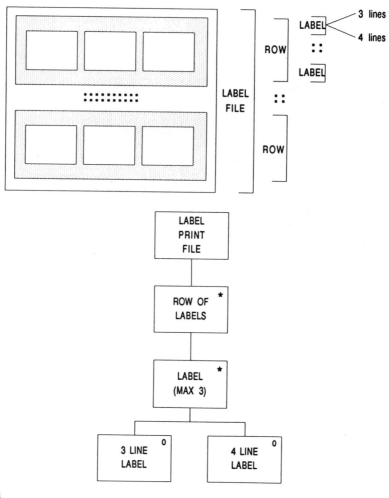

3.3.3

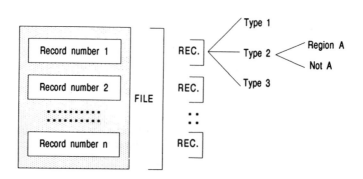

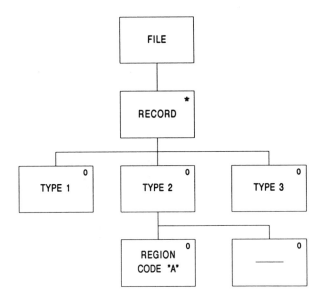

3.3.4 (a)

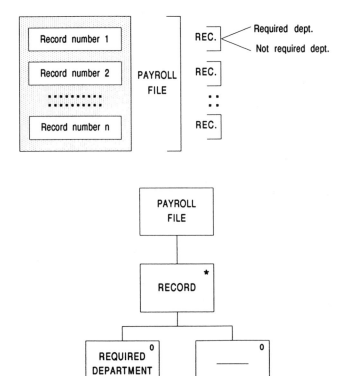

3.3.4 (b)

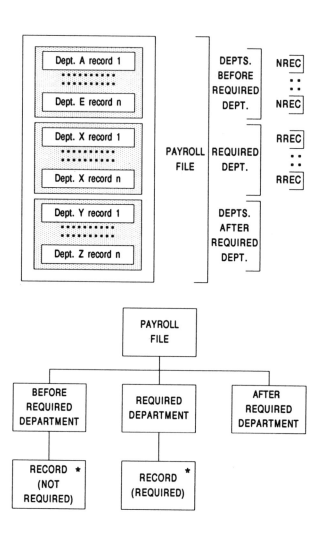

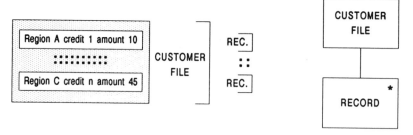

3.3.5 (a)

3.3.5 (b)

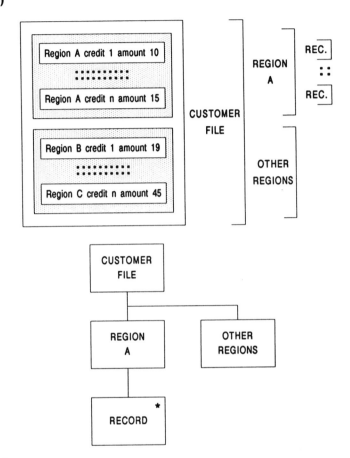

3.3.5 (c)

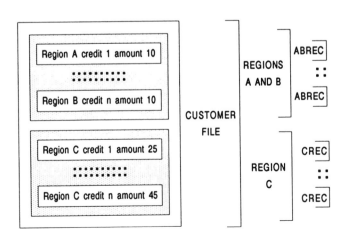

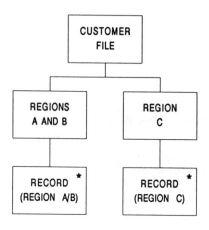

3.3.5 (d)

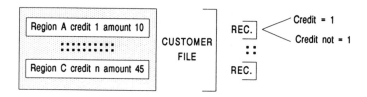

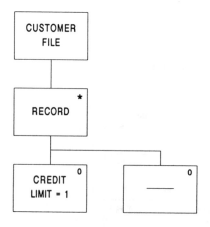

3.3.5 (e)

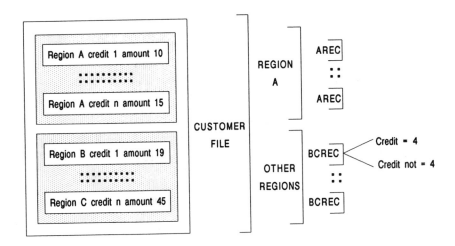

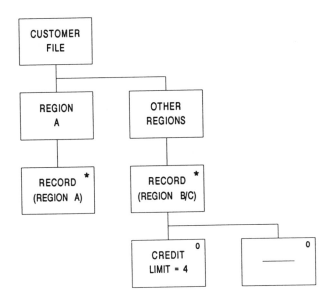

3.3.6 (a)

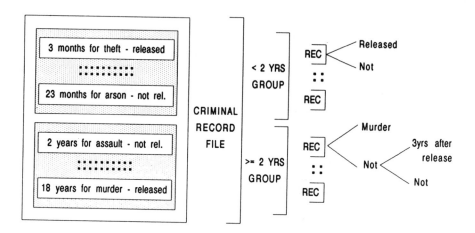

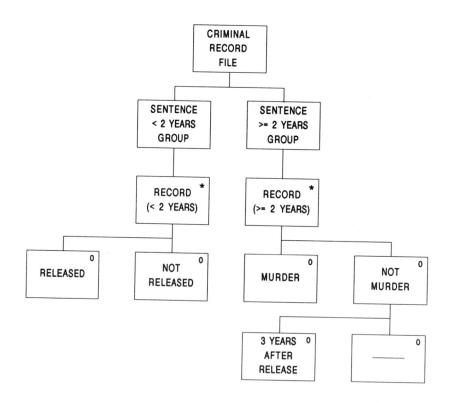

3.3.6 (b)

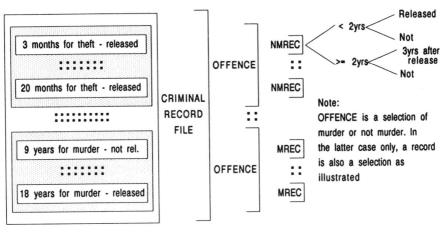

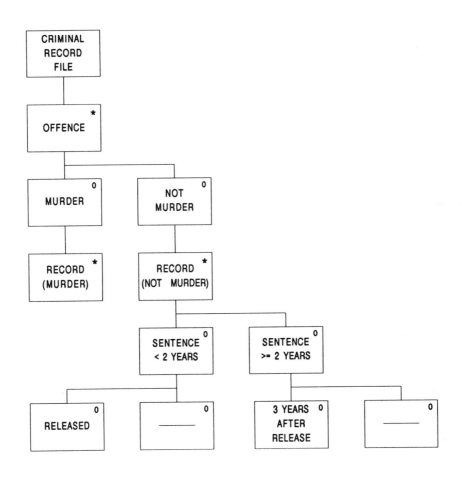

3.3.6 (c)

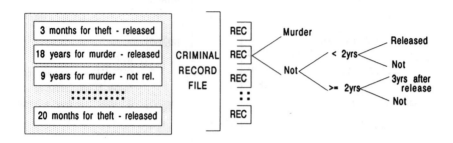

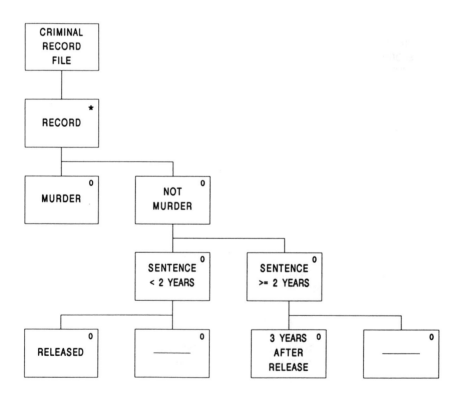

3.3.7 (a)

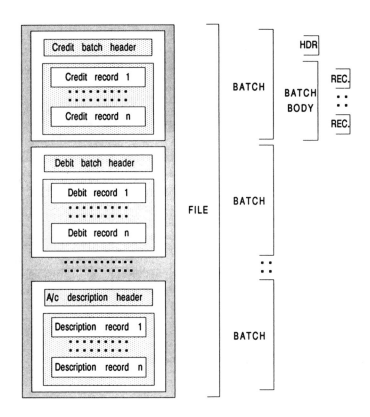

Here we note that each of the occurrences of BATCH may be a credit, a debit or an account description. Hence BATCH is a selection.

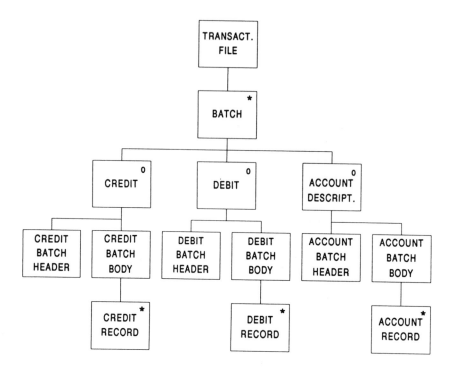

3.3.7 (b)

The component CREDIT RECORD is amended as follows:

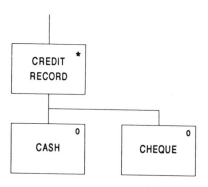

3.3.7 (c)

DEBIT BATCH BODY is amended as follows:

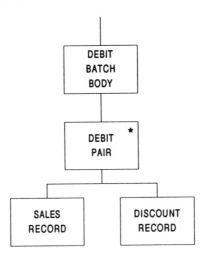

3.3.8 (a)

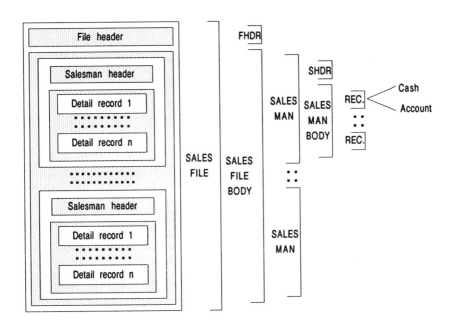

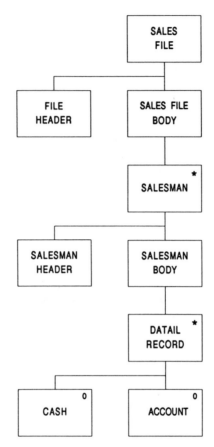

3.3.8 (b)
The component SALESMAN is amended as follows:

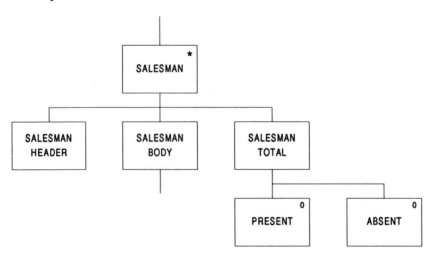

3.3.8 (c)

DETAIL RECORD is changed to:

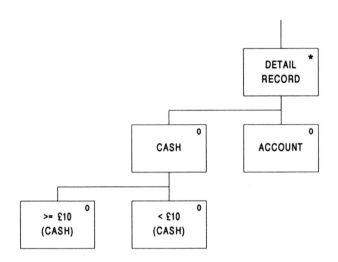

Chapter 4

4.3.1 The annotated sketch of the input file.

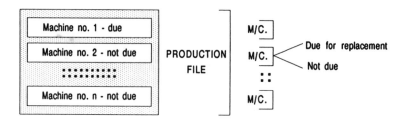

4.3.1 The annotated sketch of the output file.

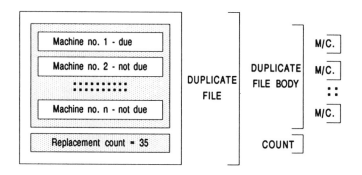

4.3.1 The logical data structures.

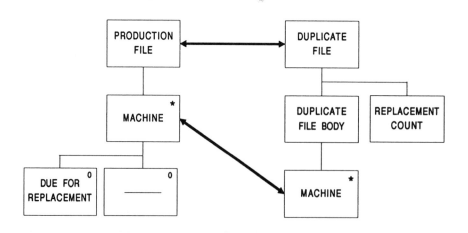

4.3.1 The program structure.

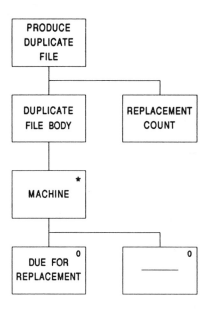

4.3.2 The annotated sketch of the input file.

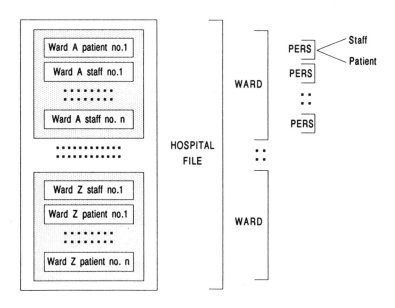

4.3.2 The annotated sketch of the output file.

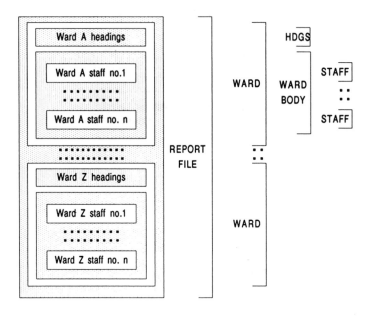

4.3.2 The logical data structures.

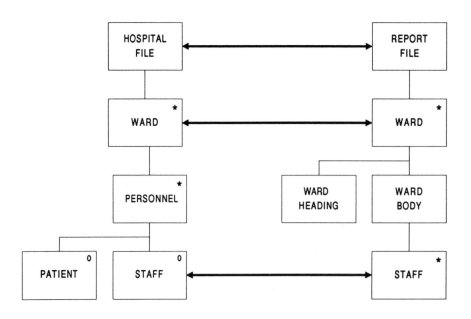

4.3.2 The program structure.

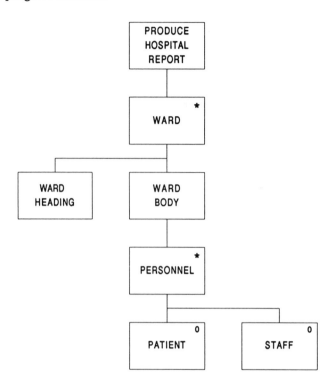

4.3.3 The annotated sketch of the input file.

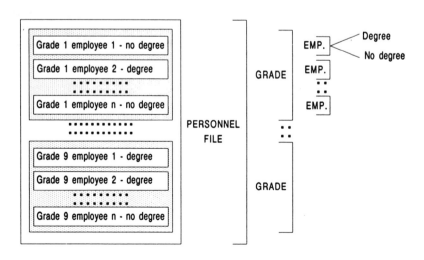

4.3.3 The annotated sketch of the output file.

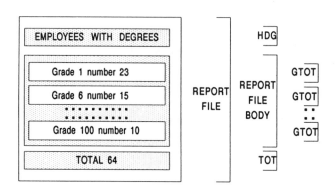

4.3.3 The logical data structures.

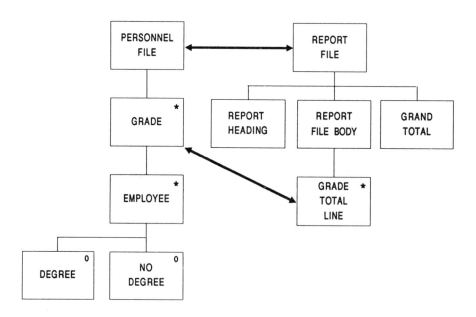

4.3.3 The program structure.

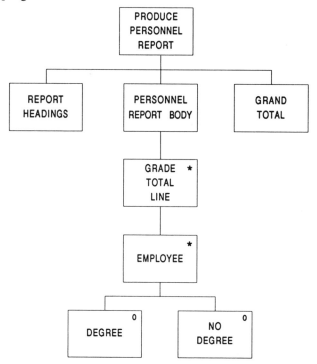

4.3.4 The annotated sketch of the output file.

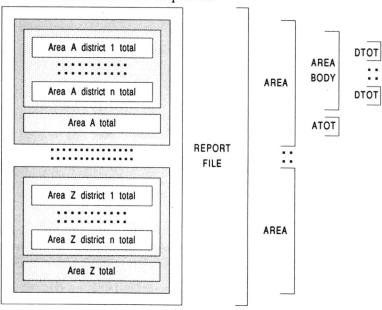

4.3.4 The annotated sketch of the input file.

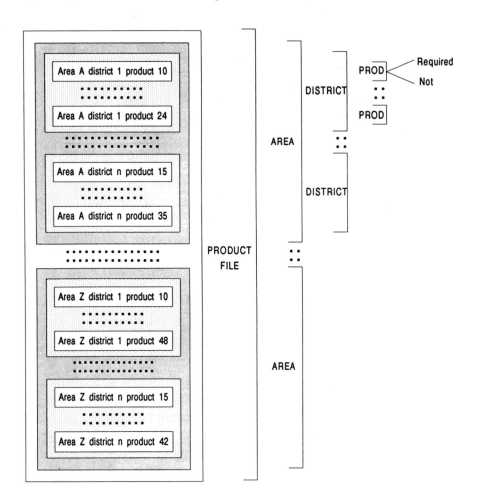

4.3.4 The logical data structures.

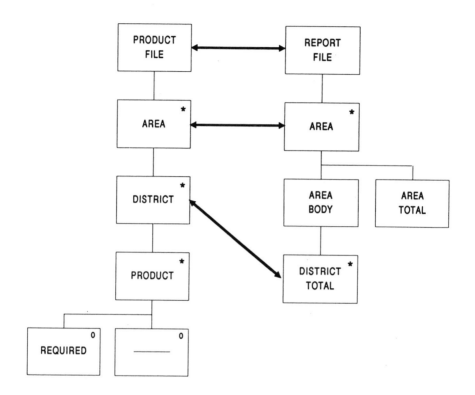

4.3.4 The program structure.

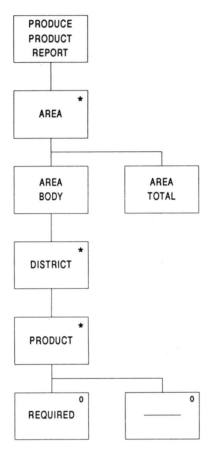

4.3.5 (a) The annotated sketch of the input file.

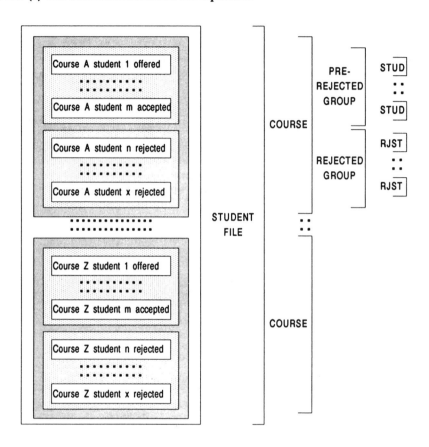

4.3.5 (a) The annotated sketch of the output file.

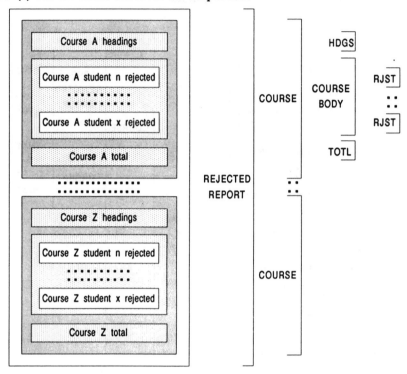

4.3.5 (a) The logical data structures.

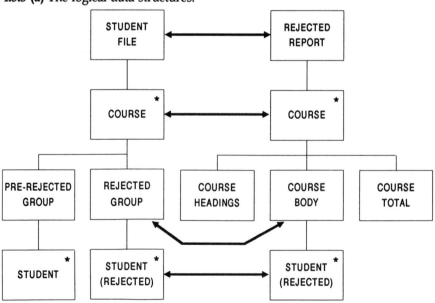

4.3.5 (a) The program structure.

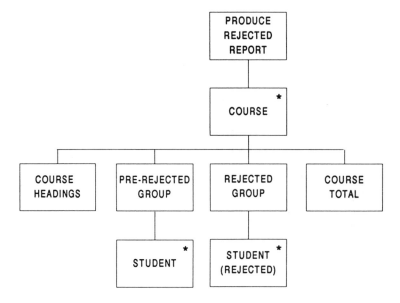

4.3.5 (b) The annotated sketch of the second output file.

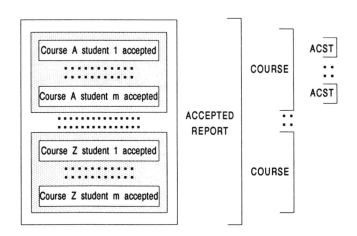

4.3.5 (b) The annotated sketch of the input file (revised).

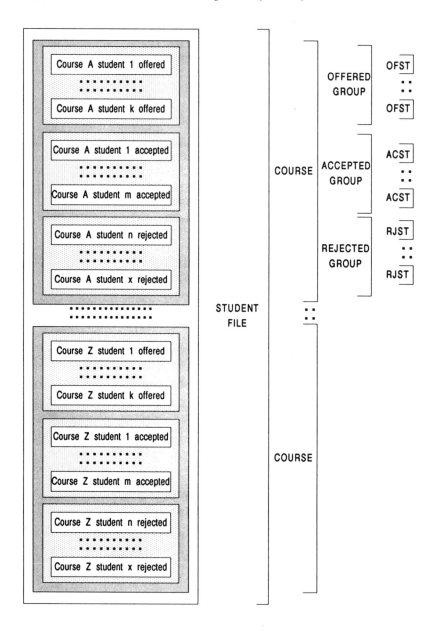

4.3.5 (b) The logical data structures.

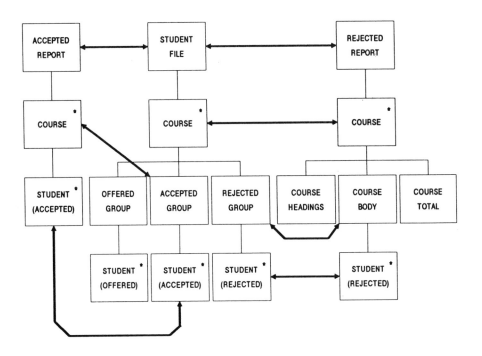

4.3.5 (b) The program structure.

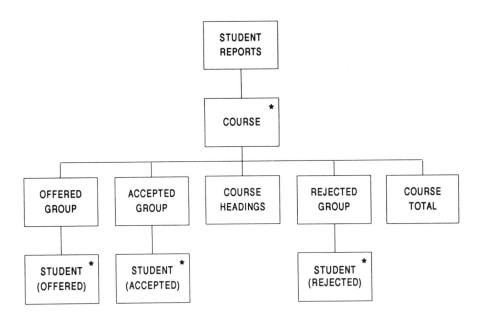

4.3.6 The annotated sketch of the input file.

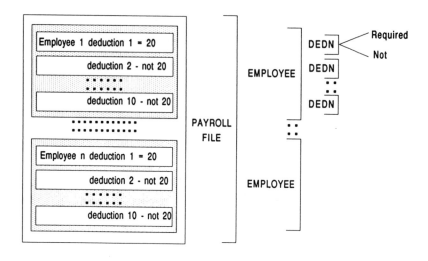

4.3.6 The annotated sketch of the output file.

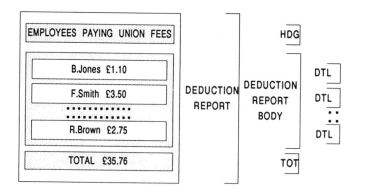

4.3.6 The logical data structures.

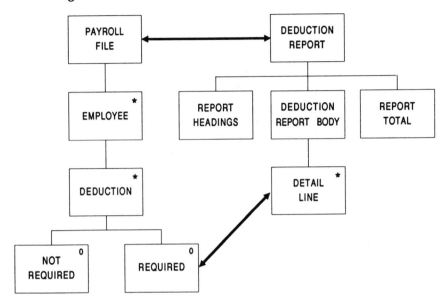

4.3.6 The program structure.

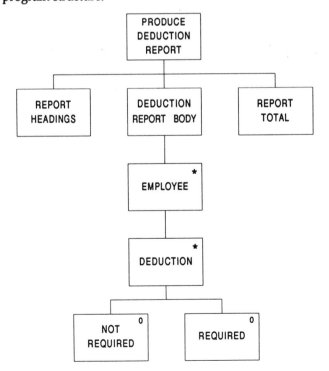

Program Design Using JSP

Chapter 5

5.4.1 (a)

C1	Until end of the input file
C2	If machine due for replacement
1	Open files
2	Close files
3	Stop
4	Read a machine record
5	Copy a machine record to output
6	Write the count record
7	Increment replacement count
8	Initialise replacement count

5.4.1 (b) - (d)

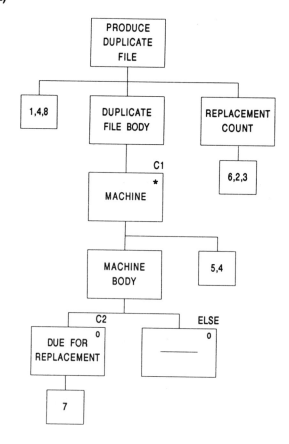

5.4.2 (a)

C1	Until end of the input file
C2	Until change of ward or end of the input file
C3	If person is a patient
1	Open files
2	Close files
3	Stop
4	Read a hospital file record
5	Print ward headings
6	Print staff name
7	Store ward

5.4.2 (b) - (d)

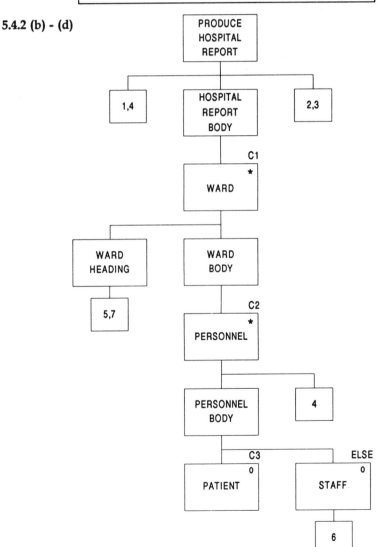

5.4.3 (a)

C1	Until end of the input file
C2	Until change of grade or end of the input file
C3	If degree = 'Y'
1	Open files
2	Close files
3	Stop
4	Read a personnel file record
5	Print report headings
6	Print grade and number line
7	Print grand total line
8	Increment degree count
9	Increment grand total
10	Initialise degree count (=0)
11	Initialise grand total (=0)
12	Store grade

5.4.3 (b) - (d)

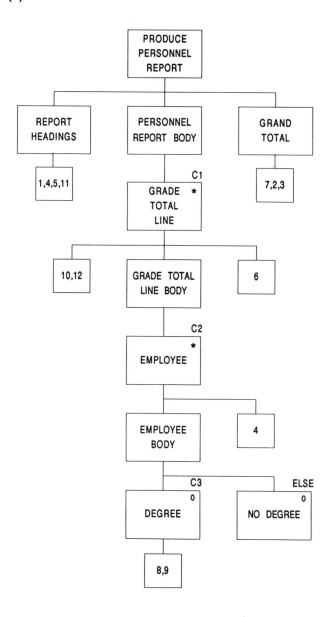

5.4.4 (a)

C1	Until end of the input file
C2	Until change of area or end of the input file
C3	Until change of district or change of area or end of the input file
C4	If product code is a required one
1	Open files
2	Close files
3	Stop
4	Read a product file record
5	Print area total line
6	Print district total line
7	Add selected value to area total
8	Add selected value to district total
9	Initialise area total
10	Initialise district total
11	Store area code
12	Store district code

5.4.4 (b) - (d)

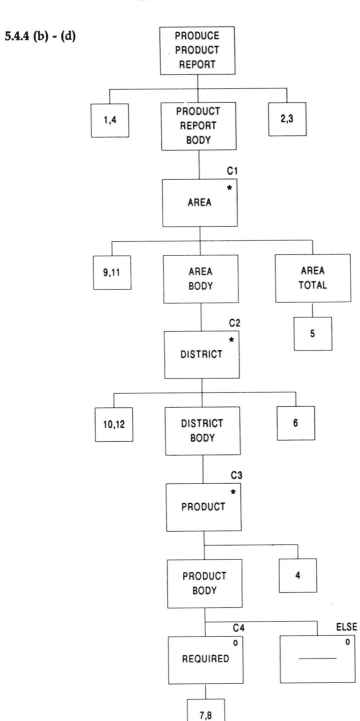

5.4.5 (a)

C1	Until end of the input file
C2	Until end of offered group or change of course or end of the input file
C3	Until end of accepted group or change of course or end of the input file
C4	Until change of course or end of the input file
1	Open files
2	Close files
3	Stop
4	Read a student file record
5	Print reject report headings
6	Print rejected student name
7	Print reject total
8	Write accepted student record
9	Increment reject total
10	Initialise reject total
11	Store course code

5.4.5 (b) - (d)

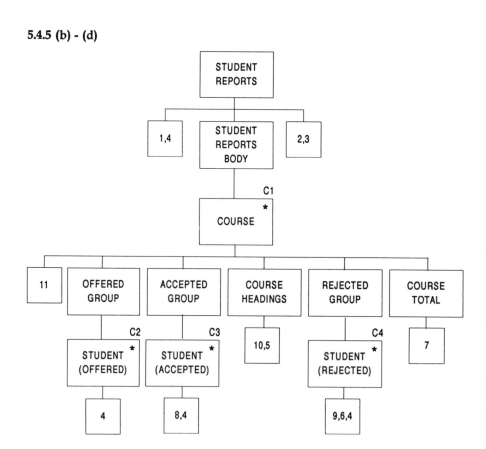

5.4.6 (a)

C1	Until end of the input file
C2	Until end of deduction group
C3	If not deduction code 20
1	Open files
2	Close files
3	Stop
4	Read a payroll file record
5	Print report headings
6	Print name and amount line
7	Print total line
8	Add deduction amount to total
9	Initialise total (=0)
10	Initialise deduction counter
11	Increment deduction counter

5.4.6 (b) - (d)

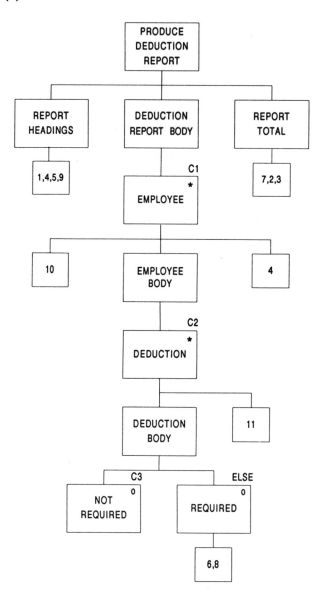

Chapter 6

6.3.1

```
PRODUCE DUPLICATE FILE SEQ
  DO 1 [Open files
  DO 4 [Read a machine record
  DO 8 [Initialise replacement count
  DUPLICATE FILE BODY ITER UNTIL C1 [end of the input file
    MACHINE SEQ
      MACHINE BODY SEL IF C2 [machine due for replacement
        DUE FOR REPLACEMENT
          DO 7 [Increment replacement count
        DUE FOR REPLACEMENT END
      MACHINE BODY ELSE 1
        [note NULL component
      MACHINE BODY END
      DO 5 [Copy a machine record to output
      DO 4 [Read a machine record
    MACHINE END
  DUPLICATE FILE BODY END
  REPLACEMENT COUNT
    DO 6 [Write the count record
    DO 2 [Close files
    DO 3 [Stop
  REPLACEMENT COUNT END
PRODUCE DUPLICATE FILE END
```

6.3.2

```
PRODUCE HOSPITAL REPORT SEQ
  DO 1 [Open files
  DO 4 [Read a hospital file record
  HOSPITAL REPORT BODY ITER UNTIL C1 [end of the input file
    WARD SEQ
      WARD HEADING
        DO 5 [Print ward headings
        DO 7 [Store ward
      WARD HEADING END
      WARD BODY ITER UNTIL C2 [change of ward or end of
                                       the input file
        PERSONNEL SEQ
          PERSONNEL BODY SEL IF C3 [person is a patient
            PATIENT
              [note - no operations for this component
            PATIENT END
          PERSONNEL BODY ELSE 1
            STAFF
              DO 6 [Print staff name
            STAFF END
          PERSONNEL BODY END
          DO 4 [Read a hospital file record
        PERSONNEL END
      WARD BODY END
    WARD END
  HOSPITAL REPORT BODY END
  DO 2 [Close files
  DO 3 [Stop
PRODUCE HOSPITAL REPORT END
```

6.3.3

```
PRODUCE PERSONNEL REPORT SEQ
  REPORT HEADINGS
    DO 1  [Open files
    DO 4  [Read a personnel file record
    DO 5  [Print report headings
    DO 11 [Initialise grand total (=0)
  REPORT HEADINGS END
  PERSONNEL REPORT BODY ITER UNTIL C1 [end of the input file
    GRADE TOTAL LINE SEQ
      DO 10 [Initialise degree count (=0)
      DO 12 [Store grade
      GRADE TOTAL LINE BODY ITER UNTIL C2 [change of grade or
                                              end of input file
        EMPLOYEE SEQ
          EMPLOYEE BODY SEL IF C3 [degree = 'Y'
            DEGREE
              DO 8 [Increment degree count
              DO 9 [Increment grand total
            DEGREE END
          EMPLOYEE BODY ELSE 1
            NO DEGREE
              [note - no operations for this component
            NO DEGREE END
          EMPLOYEE BODY END
          DO 4 [Read a personnel file record
        EMPLOYEE END
      GRADE TOTAL LINE BODY END
      DO 6 [Print grade and number line
    GRADE TOTAL LINE END
  PERSONNEL REPORT BODY END
  GRAND TOTAL
    DO 7 [Print grand total line
    DO 2 [Close files
    DO 3 [Stop
  GRAND TOTAL END
PRODUCE PERSONNEL REPORT END
```

6.3.4

```
PRODUCE PRODUCT REPORT SEQ
  DO 1 [Open files
  DO 4 [Read a product file record
  PRODUCT REPORT BODY ITER UNTIL C1 [end of the input file
    AREA SEQ
      DO 9  [Initialise area total
      DO 11 [Store area code
      AREA BODY ITER UNTIL C2 [change of area or end of the
                                       input file
        DISTRICT SEQ
          DO 10 [Initialise district total
          DO 12 [Store district code
          DISTRICT BODY ITER UNTIL C3 [change of district or
                        change of area or end of the input file
            PRODUCT SEQ
              PRODUCT BODY SEL IF C4 [product code is a
                                       required one
                REQUIRED
                  DO 7 [Add selected value to area total
                  DO 8 [Add selected value to district total
                REQUIRED END
              PRODUCT BODY ELSE 1
                [note NULL component
              PRODUCT BODY END
              DO 4 [Read a product file record
            PRODUCT END
          DISTRICT BODY END
          DO 6 [Print district total line
        DISTRICT END
      AREA BODY END
      AREA TOTAL
        DO 5 [Print area total line
      AREA TOTAL END
    AREA END
  PRODUCT REPORT BODY END
  DO 2 [Close files
  DO 3 [Stop
PRODUCE PRODUCT REPORT END
```

6.3.5

```
STUDENT REPORTS SEQ
  DO 1 [Open files
  DO 4 [Read a student file record
  STUDENT REPORTS BODY ITER UNTIL C1 [end of the input file
    COURSE SEQ
      DO 11 [Store course code
      OFFERED GROUP ITER UNTIL C2 [end of offered group or
                          change of course or end of the input file
        STUDENT (OFFERED)
          DO 4 [Read a student file record
        STUDENT (OFFERED) END
      OFFERED GROUP END
      ACCEPTED GROUP ITER UNTIL C3 [end of accepted group or
                          change of course or end of the input file
        STUDENT (ACCEPTED)
          DO 8 [Write accepted student record
          DO 4 [Read a student file record
        STUDENT (ACCEPTED) END
      ACCEPTED GROUP END
      COURSE HEADINGS
        DO 10 [Initialise reject total
        DO 5  [Print reject report headings
      COURSE HEADINGS END
      REJECTED GROUP ITER UNTIL C4 [change of course or
                                    end of the input file
        STUDENT (REJECTED)
          DO 9 [Increment reject total
          DO 6 [Print rejected student name
          DO 4 [Read a student file record
        STUDENT (REJECTED) END
      REJECTED GROUP END
      COURSE TOTAL
        DO 7 [Print reject total
      COURSE TOTAL END
    COURSE END
  STUDENT REPORTS BODY END
  DO 2 [Close files
  DO 3 [Stop
STUDENT REPORTS END
```

6.3.6

```
PRODUCE DEDUCTION REPORT SEQ
   REPORT HEADINGS
      DO 1 [Open files
      DO 4 [Read a payroll file record
      DO 5 [Print report headings
      DO 9 [Initialise total (=0)
   REPORT HEADINGS END
   DEDUCTION REPORT BODY ITER UNTIL C1 [end of the input file
      EMPLOYEE SEQ
         DO 10 [Initialise deduction counter
         EMPLOYEE BODY ITER UNTIL C2 [end of deduction group
            DEDUCTION SEQ
               DEDUCTION BODY SEL IF C3 [not deduction code 20
                  NOT REQUIRED
                     [note no operations
                  NOT REQUIRED END
               DEDUCTION BODY ELSE 1
                  REQUIRED
                     DO 6 [Print name and amount line
                     DO 8 [Add deduction amount to total
                  REQUIRED END
               DEDUCTION BODY END
               DO 11 [Increment deduction counter
            DEDUCTION END
         EMPLOYEE BODY END
         DO 4 [Read a payroll file record
      EMPLOYEE END
   DEDUCTION REPORT BODY END
   REPORT TOTAL
      DO 7 [Print total line
      DO 2 [Close files
      DO 3 [Stop
   REPORT TOTAL END
PRODUCE DEDUCTION REPORT END
```

Chapter 7

7.4.1

```
IDENTIFICATION DIVISION.
PROGRAM-ID. MACHINES.
ENVIRONMENT DIVISION.
INPUT-OUTPUT SECTION.
FILE-CONTROL.
    SELECT OLD-FILE ASSIGN TO "PRODFILE.INP".
    SELECT NEW-FILE ASSIGN TO "DUPFILE.OUT".
DATA DIVISION.
FILE SECTION.
FD  OLD-FILE.
01  PRODUCTION-RECORD.
        03 RECORD-TYPE          PIC 9.
           88 END-OF-FILE        VALUE 9.
        03 MACHINE              PIC X(20).
        03 DATE-PURCHASED       PIC X(8).
        03 REPLACEMENT          PIC 9.
           88 REPLACEMENT-DUE    VALUE 9.
FD  NEW-FILE.
01  NEW-PRODUCTION-RECORD       PIC X(30).
WORKING-STORAGE SECTION.
01  COUNT-RECORD.
        03 FILLER               PIC 9
                                VALUE 8.
        03 REPLACE-COUNT        PIC 9(6).
PROCEDURE DIVISION.
PRODUCE-DUPLICATE-FILE-SEQ.
    OPEN INPUT OLD-FILE OUTPUT NEW-FILE.
    READ OLD-FILE AT END MOVE 9 TO RECORD-TYPE.
    MOVE 0 TO REPLACE-COUNT.
DUPLICATE-FILE-BODY-ITER.
    IF END-OF-FILE GO TO DUPLICATE-FILE-BODY-END.
MACHINE-SEQ.
MACHINE-BODY-SEL.
    IF REPLACEMENT-DUE NEXT SENTENCE
        ELSE GO TO MACHINE-BODY-ELSE-1.
DUE-FOR-REPLACEMENT.
    ADD 1 TO REPLACE-COUNT.
DUE-FOR-REPLACEMENT-END.
    GO TO MACHINE-BODY-END.
MACHINE-BODY-ELSE-1.
** null component **
MACHINE-BODY-END.
    WRITE NEW-PRODUCTION-RECORD FROM PRODUCTION-RECORD.
    READ OLD-FILE AT END MOVE 9 TO RECORD-TYPE.
MACHINE-END.
    GO TO DUPLICATE-FILE-BODY-ITER.
DUPLICATE-FILE-BODY-END.
REPLACEMENT-COUNT.
    WRITE NEW-PRODUCTION-RECORD FROM COUNT-RECORD.
    CLOSE OLD-FILE NEW-FILE.
    STOP RUN.
REPLACEMENT-COUNT-END.
PRODUCE-DUPLICATE-FILE-END.
```

7.4.2

```
PROGRAM Hospital (hospfile, staffile) ;
TYPE
   packed4       = PACKED ARRAY [1..4] OF char ;
   recordtype    = RECORD
                         ward    : packed4 ;
                         name    : PACKED ARRAY [1..20] OF char ;
                         patient : boolean ;
                     END ;
VAR
   storedward     : packed4 ;
   hosprecord     : recordtype ;
   hospfile       : FILE OF recordtype ;
   staffile       : text ;
BEGIN
(* produce hospital report seq *)
  Reset (hospfile) ;
  Rewrite (staffile) ;
  Read (hospfile, hosprecord) ;
  WITH hosprecord DO
  (* hospital report body iter *)
  WHILE NOT (ward = 'ZZZZ') DO
    BEGIN
    (* ward seq *)
      (* ward heading *)
        Writeln (staffile, 'STAFF ON WARD ', ward) ;
        Writeln (staffile) ;
        storedward := ward ;
      (* ward heading end *)
      (* ward body iter *)
      WHILE NOT ((ward = 'ZZZZ') OR (ward <> storedward)) DO
        BEGIN
        (* personnel seq *)
          (* personnel body sel *)
          IF patient THEN
            (* patient *)
              (* no operations for this component *)
            (* patient end *)
          (* personnel body else 1 *)
          ELSE
            (* staff *)
              Writeln (staffile, name) ;
            (* staff end *)
          (* personnel body end *)
          Read (hospfile, hosprecord) ;
        (* personnel end *)
        END ;
      (* ward body end *)
    (* ward end *)
    END ;
  (* hospital report body end *)
(* produce hospital report end *)
END.
```

7.4.3

```
IDENTIFICATION DIVISION.
PROGRAM-ID. PERSON.
ENVIRONMENT DIVISION.
INPUT-OUTPUT SECTION.
FILE-CONTROL.
    SELECT PERSONNEL-FILE ASSIGN TO "PERSON.SEQ".
    SELECT OUTPUT-REPORT-FILE ASSIGN TO "REPORT.LPT".
DATA DIVISION.
FILE SECTION.
FD  PERSONNEL-FILE.
01  PERSONNEL-REC.
    03 GRADE                  PIC 999.
    03 NAME                   PIC X(17).
    03 O-LEVELS               PIC 9.
    03 A-LEVELS               PIC 9.
    03 DEGREE-Y-N             PIC X.
       88 HAS-DEGREE          VALUE "Y".
FD  OUTPUT-REPORT-FILE.
01  PRINT-LINE                PIC X(80).
WORKING-STORAGE SECTION.
01  MAIN-HEADINGS             PIC X(36) VALUE
    "XYZ COMPANY - EMPLOYEES WITH DEGREES".
01  SUB-HEADINGS              PIC X(24) VALUE
    "     GRADE      NUMBER".
01  DETAIL-LINE.
    03 FILLER                 PIC X(7)  VALUE SPACES.
    03 OUT-GRADE              PIC ZZ9.
    03 FILLER                 PIC X(7)  VALUE SPACES.
    03 OUT-DEGREE-COUNT       PIC ZZZ9.
01  TOTAL-LINE.
    03 FILLER                 PIC X(16) VALUE "        TOTAL".
    03 OUT-GRAND-TOTAL-COUNT  PIC ZZZZ9.
77  DEGREE-COUNT             PIC 9(4).
77  GRAND-TOTAL-COUNT        PIC 9(5).
77  STORED-GRADE             PIC 999.
PROCEDURE DIVISION.
PRODUCE-PERSONNEL-REPORT-SEQ.
REPORT-HEADINGS.
    OPEN INPUT PERSONNEL-FILE OUTPUT OUTPUT-REPORT-FILE.
    READ PERSONNEL-FILE AT END MOVE 999 TO GRADE.
    WRITE PRINT-LINE FROM MAIN-HEADINGS
    WRITE PRINT-LINE FROM SUB-HEADINGS AFTER 1
    WRITE PRINT-LINE FROM SPACES AFTER 1.
    MOVE ZERO TO GRAND-TOTAL-COUNT.
REPORT-HEADINGS-END.
PERSONNEL-REPORT-BODY-ITER.
    IF GRADE = 999 GO TO PERSONNEL-REPORT-BODY-END.
GRADE-TOTAL-LINE-SEQ.
    MOVE ZERO TO DEGREE-COUNT.
    MOVE GRADE TO STORED-GRADE.
GRADE-TOTAL-LINE-BODY-ITER.
    IF GRADE = 999 OR GRADE NOT = STORED-GRADE
        GO TO GRADE-TOTAL-LINE-BODY-END.
EMPLOYEE-SEQ.
EMPLOYEE-BODY-SEL.
    IF HAS-DEGREE NEXT SENTENCE
        ELSE GO TO EMPLOYEE-BODY-ELSE-1.
```

```
DEGREE.
    ADD 1 TO DEGREE-COUNT.
    ADD 1 TO GRAND-TOTAL-COUNT.
DEGREE-END.
    GO TO EMPLOYEE-BODY-END.
EMPLOYEE-BODY-ELSE-1.
NO-DEGREE.
** NO OPERATIONS FOR THIS COMPONENT **
NO-DEGREE-END.
EMPLOYEE-BODY-END.
    READ PERSONNEL-FILE AT END MOVE 999 TO GRADE.
EMPLOYEE-END.
    GO TO GRADE-TOTAL-LINE-BODY-ITER.
GRADE-TOTAL-LINE-BODY-END.
    MOVE STORED-GRADE TO OUT-GRADE
    MOVE DEGREE-COUNT TO OUT-DEGREE-COUNT
    WRITE PRINT-LINE FROM DETAIL-LINE.
GRADE-TOTAL-LINE-END.
    GO TO PERSONNEL-REPORT-BODY-ITER.
PERSONNEL-REPORT-BODY-END.
GRAND-TOTAL.
    MOVE GRAND-TOTAL-COUNT TO OUT-GRAND-TOTAL-COUNT
    WRITE PRINT-LINE FROM TOTAL-LINE.
    CLOSE PERSONNEL-FILE OUTPUT-REPORT-FILE.
    STOP RUN.
GRAND-TOTAL-END.
PRODUCE-PERSONNEL-REPORT-END.
```

Chapter 8

8.4.1

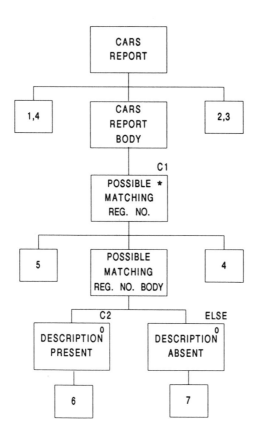

C1	Until end of CARS SOLD file
C2	If record found in CARS FOR SALE file (direct access)
1	Open files
2	Close files
3	Stop
4	Read a CARS SOLD file record
5	Attempt to access CARS FOR SALE file record with registration number = that in CARS SOLD file record
6	Print car description
7	Print 'description not known'

8.4.2

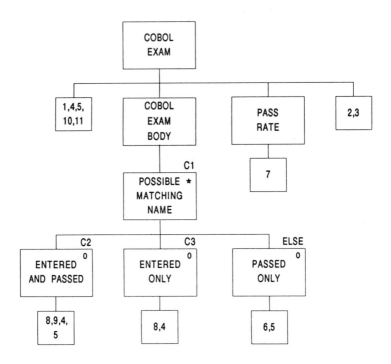

C1	Until end of both input files
C2	If ENTERED name = PASSED name
C3	If ENTERED name < PASSED name
1	Open files
2	Close files
3	Stop
4	Read ENTERED file record
5	Read PASSED file record
6	Print passed/not entered name
7	Compute and print pass rate
8	Increment entered count
9	Increment passed count
10	Initialise entered count
11	Initialise passed count

8.4.3

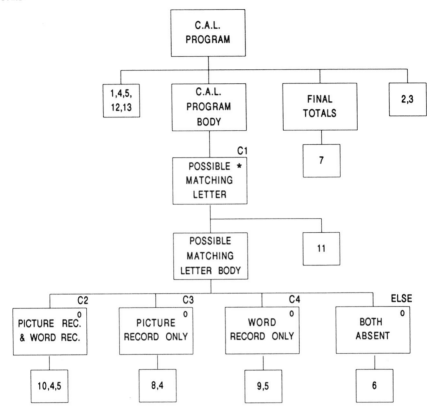

C1	Until end of letter range
C2	If current letter = PICTURE file letter = WORD file letter
C3	If current letter = PICTURE file letter <> WORD file letter
C4	If current letter = WORD file letter <> PICTURE file letter
1	Open files
2	Close files
3	Stop
4	Read PICTURE file record
5	Read WORD file record
6	Print appropriate initial letter
7	Compute and print percentages
8	Increment picture only total
9	Increment word only total
10	Increment picture with word total
11	Increment current letter (move to next in alphabet)
12	Initialise all totals
13	Initialise current letter (= A)

8.4.4

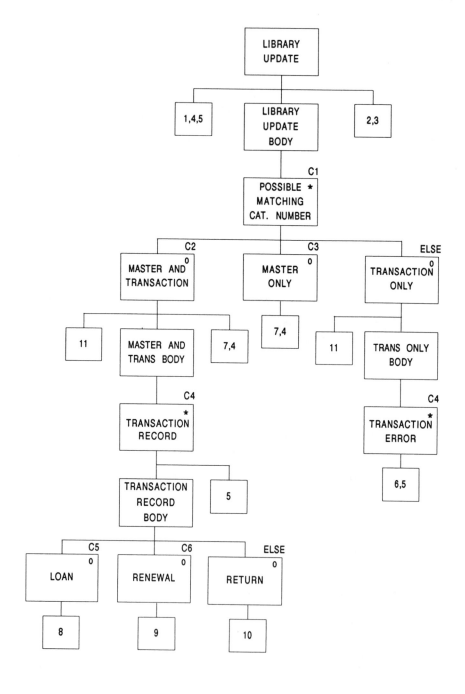

In this solution we have simplified the component TRANSACTION ERROR. Strictly, it should contain the same structure as that for TRANSACTION RECORD BODY. However, the only operation to be allocated to each of the three selection part components would be number 6, display 'transaction alone' error message.

C1	Until end of both input files
C2	If MASTER catalogue number = TRANSACTION catalogue number
C3	If MASTER catalogue number < TRANSACTION catalogue number
C4	Until change of TRANSACTION catalogue number
C5	If CODE = 1
C6	If CODE = 2
1	Open files
2	Close files
3	Stop
4	Read MASTER file record
5	Read TRANSACTION file record
6	Display 'transaction alone' error message
7	Write master record to output
8	Update borrower's reference and date in master record
9	Update date in master record
10	Space-fill borrower's reference in master record
11	Store TRANSACTION catalogue number

Chapter 9

9.7.1

operation	inter. status	entry status	intermediate file record type	contents		
2	0 (False)					
7			DETAIL	MATHS	F JONES	35
21						
26 (1st)						
26 (2nd)		2				
7			DETAIL	MATHS	C DODD	48
26 (2nd)		2				
8			TOTAL	MATHS		83
26 (2nd)		2				
7			DETAIL	SCIENCE	J BROWN	62
26 (2nd)		2				
8			TOTAL	SCIENCE		62
26 (2nd)		2				
4	1 (True)		NULL	NULL		
24						
25						

In Pascal, entry status is initialised to 1 at the start of the main program. In COBOL it is initialised to 1 in the WORKING-STORAGE of the subprogram.

9.7.2 (a)

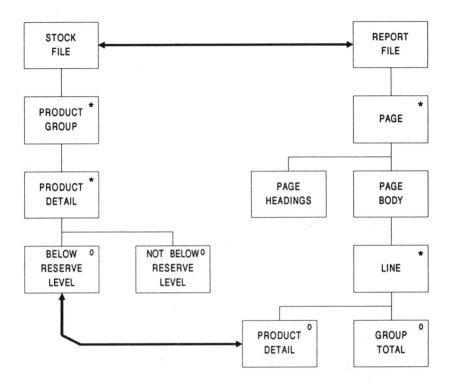

A structure clash exists between PRODUCT GROUP and PAGE.

9.7.2 (b) Data structures (program 1)

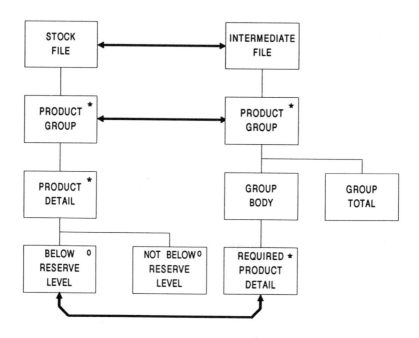

9.7.2 (b) Condition and operation lists (program 1)

C1	Until end of stock file
C2	Until change of product group or end of stock file
C3	If stock level < 20
1	Open stock file
2	Open intermediate file
3	Close stock file
4	Close intermediate file
5	Stop
6	Read a stock file record
7	Write detail record to intermediate file
8	Write total record to intermediate file
9	Increment group total
10	Initialise group total (=0)
11	Store product group code

9.7.2 (b) Program structure (program 1)

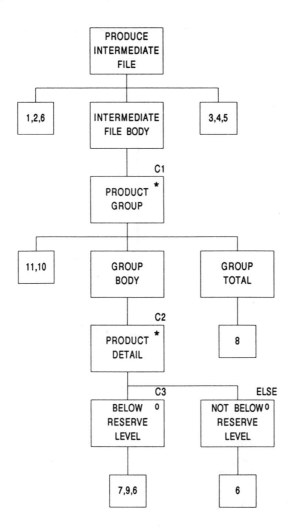

9.7.2 (c) Data structures (program 2)

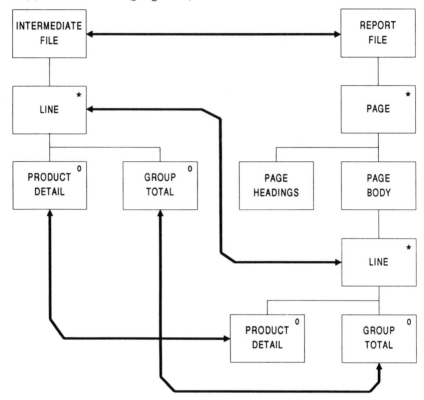

9.7.2 (c) Condition and operation lists (program 2)

C1	Until end of intermediate file
C2	Until end of page or end of intermediate file
C3	If a product detail line
1	Open intermediate file
2	Open report file
3	Close report file
4	Close intermediate file
5	Stop
6	Read an intermediate file record
7	Print page headings
8	Print detail line
9	Print total line
10	Increment line count
11	Increment page count
12	Initialise line count (=0)
13	Initialise page count (=0)

9.7.2 (c) Program structure (program 2)

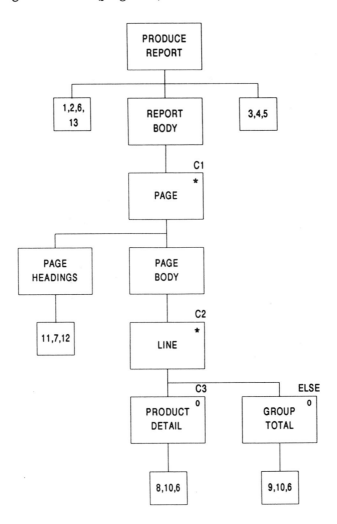

9.7.2 (d)

Use the rules from section 9.5 to code operations 2, 4, 7 and 8 from program 1, and operations 1, 4, 5 and 6 from program 2.

Initialise entry status and include code at the beginning of program 2 for the control passing mechanism.

Chapter 10

10.7.1 Data structures

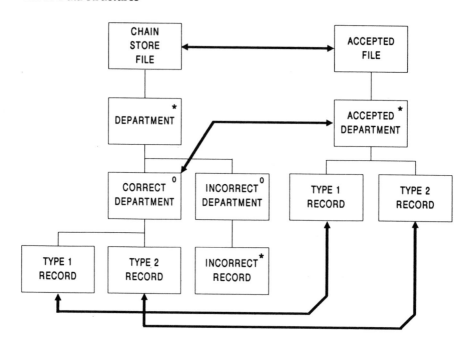

10.7.1 The initial condition and operation lists

C1	Until end of chain store file
C2	Until change of department or end of chain store file
1	Open files
2	Close file
3	Stop
4	Read a chain store file record
5	Write a type 1 record
6	Write a type 2 record
7	Display error message
8	Store department code

10.7.1 The program structure with allocated operations and conditions

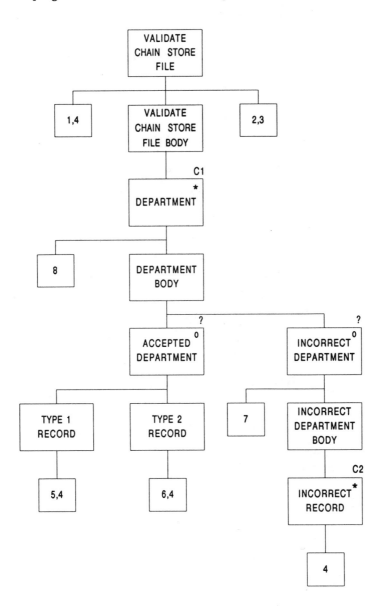

10.7.1 The final schematic logic

```
VALIDATE CHAIN STORE FILE SEQ
  DO 1  [Open files
  DO 4  [Read a chain store file record
  VALIDATE CHAIN STORE FILE BODY ITER UNTIL C1 [end of chain
                                              store file
    DEPARTMENT SEQ
      DO 8  [Store department code
      DEPARTMENT BODY POSIT (a good department)
        ACCEPTED DEPARTMENT SEQ
          TYPE 1 RECORD
            QUIT DEPARTMENT BODY POSIT IF C3 [record not a type 1
                                    or cash value out of range
            DO 5  [Store a type 1 record **
            DO 4  [Read a chain store file record
            QUIT DEPARTMENT BODY POSIT IF C4 [not the same
                                department or not a type 2 record
          TYPE 1 RECORD END
          TYPE 2 RECORD
            QUIT DEPARTMENT BODY POSIT IF C5 [cash value out of
                 range or end of day cash not > start of day cash
            DO 6  [Store a type 2 record **
            DO 4  [Read a chain store file record
            QUIT DEPARTMENT BODY POSIT IF C6 [same department
          TYPE 2 RECORD END
          DO 5A  [Write stored type 1 record **
          DO 6A  [Write stored type 2 record **
        ACCEPTED DEPARTMENT END
      DEPARTMENT BODY ADMIT (an incorrect department)
        INCORRECT DEPARTMENT SEQ
          DO 7  [Display error message
          INCORRECT DEPARTMENT BODY ITER UNTIL C2 [change of
                                    department or end of file
            INCORRECT RECORD
              DO 4  [Read a chain store file record
            INCORRECT RECORD END
          INCORRECT DEPARTMENT BODY END
        INCORRECT DEPARTMENT END
      DEPARTMENT BODY END
    DEPARTMENT END
  VALIDATE CHAIN STORE FILE BODY END
  DO 2  [Close files
  DO 3  [Stop
VALIDATE CHAIN STORE FILE END
```

Note that both occurrences of operation 4 (in TYPE 1 RECORD and TYPE 2 RECORD) are favourable. Operations 5 and 6 have been changed from write operations to store operations in order to overcome intolerable side effects. Operations 5A and 6A are the postponed write operations (from stored areas), implemented after all QUITs.

Chapter 12

12.6.1 The menu selection process program structure

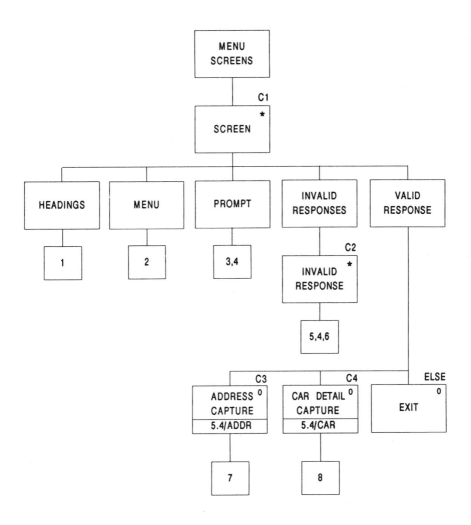

C1	Until user chooses 'exit'
C2	Until a valid response
C3	If user chooses 'address details'
C4	If user chooses 'car details'

1	Display headings on clear screen
2	Display menu lines
3	Display selection prompt
4	Accept user response
5	Display error message (try again)
6	Clear error message
7	Call address capture subprogram (see below)
8	Call car details capture subprogram (see below)

To implement QUIT from iteration at the schematic logic stage: remove condition C1 from the head of the iteration MENU SCREENS. Allocate QUIT MENU SCREENS ITER to the component EXIT.

12.6.1 The address capture process program structure

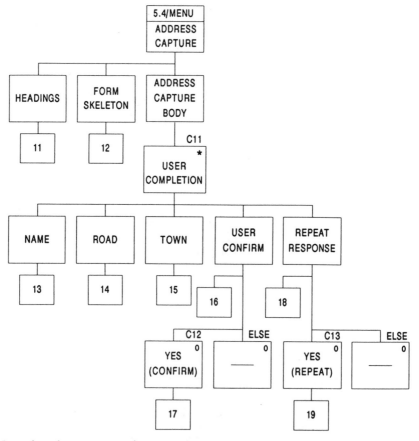

Note that the structure diagram should be redrawn to include 'body' boxes after operations 16 and 18.

C11	Until repeat response <> 'Y'
C12	If user confirmation affirmative
C13	If repeat response affirmative
11	Display headings on clear screen
12	Display form skeleton
13	Accept name
14	Accept road
15	Accept town
16	Accept user confirmation
17	Write accepted data
18	Accept repeat response
19	Clear form entries

To implement a QUIT from iteration: remove C11 from the head of the iteration ADDRESS CAPTURE BODY and allocate QUIT ADDRESS CAPTURE BODY ITER to the ELSE component of REPEAT RESPONSE BODY.

12.6.1 The car details capture process program structure

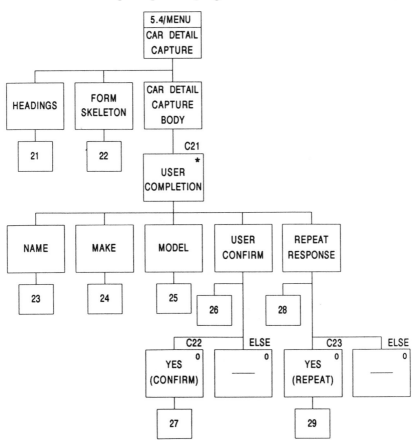

Note that the structure diagram should be redrawn to include 'body' boxes after operations 26 and 28.

C21	Until repeat response <> 'Y'
C22	If user confirmation affirmative
C23	If repeat response affirmative
21	Display headings on clear screen
22	Display form skeleton
23	Accept name
24	Accept make
25	Accept model
26	Accept user confirmation
27	Write accepted data
28	Accept repeat response
29	Clear form entries

We may employ QUIT from iteration in a similar manner to that described for the address capture subprogram.

12.6.2

C1	Until user requests no more (another name response <> 'Y')
C2	If record for required name found (that is, valid)
C3	Until user requests no more (another field response <> 'Y')
C4	If field = 'MAKE'
C5	If field = 'MODEL'
1	Display 'which person?' prompt
2	Accept user response (name)
3	Attempt to retrieve required record
4	Display 'does not exist'
5	Display 'which field?' prompt
6	Accept user response (field name)
7	Display make of car
8	Display model of car
9	Display 'try another field' prompt
10	Accept user response (another field)
11	Display 'try another name' prompt
12	Accept user response (another name)
13	Display 'exit'
14	Initialise another name response = Y
15	Initialise another field response = Y

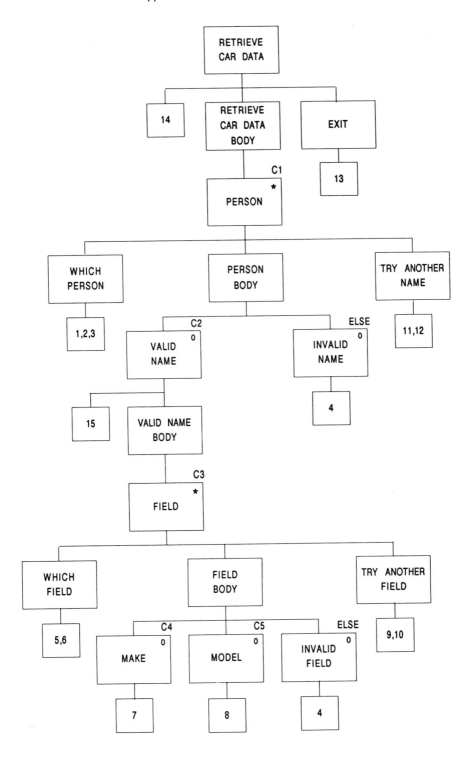

Chapter 13

13.5.1

The expected results are:

Headings for ward A100
Staff name B C WHITE
Headings for ward B300
Staff name A B GREEN

OPERATIONS/ CONDITIONS	CURRENT RECORD WARD	CURRENT RECORD NAME	P/S	STORED WARD	OUTPUT (RESULTS)
1					
4	A100	J G SMITH	P		
C1 (false)					
5					✓
7				A100	
C2 (false)					
C3 (true)					
4	A100	J L THOMAS	P		
C2 (false)					
C3 (true)					
4	A100	B C WHITE	S		
C2 (false)					
C3 (false)					
6					✓
4	B300	A B GREEN	S		
C2 (true)					
C1 (false)					
5					✓
7				B300	
C2 (false)					
C3 (false)					
6					✓
4	----	END OF FILE	----		
C2 (true)					
C1 (true)					
2					
3					

13.5.2

The expected results are:

Present on both 2, A only 1, B only 0

OPERATIONS/ CONDITIONS	A RECORD	B RECORD	A ONLY COUNT	B ONLY COUNT	BOTH COUNT	OUTPUT (RESULTS)
1						
4	1235					
5		1468				
12			0	0	0	
C1 (false)						
C2 (false)						
C3 (true)						
8			1			
4	1468					
C1 (false)						
C2 (true)						
7					1	
4	1532					
5		1532				
C1 (false)						
C2 (true)						
7					2	
4	9999					
5		9999				
C1 (true)						
6						✓
2						
3						

The test data are insufficient because the ELSE path of the selection POSSIBLE MATCHING KEY has not been used and hence operations 9 and 5 of the elementary component FILE B ONLY have not been tested.

13.5.3 (a)

path 1	C1, C2∩C3, $\overline{C1}$
path 2	$\overline{C1}$

13.5.3 (b)

path 1	C1, C2∩C1, C3, $\overline{C1}$
path 2	C1, C2∩C1, C4, $\overline{C1}$
path 3	C5
path 4	C6

13.5.3 (c)

Using De Morgan's law, we get:

$$\text{C1 (C2}\cup\text{C3) } (\overline{\text{C4}}\cap\overline{\text{C5}})$$

This gives the following paths:

path 1	C1, C2, $\overline{\text{C4}}\cap\overline{\text{C5}}$
path 2	C1, C3, $\overline{\text{C4}}\cap\overline{\text{C5}}$

13.5.3 (d)

Using De Morgan's law, we get:

$$\text{C1 } (\overline{\text{C2}}\cup\overline{\text{C3}}) \text{ (C7}\cap\text{C8) (C4}\cup\text{C5) } \overline{\text{C1}} \cup \overline{\text{C1}}$$

This gives the following paths:

path 1	C1, $\overline{\text{C2}}$, C7∩C8, C4, $\overline{\text{C1}}$
path 2	C1, $\overline{\text{C3}}$, C7∩C8, C4, $\overline{\text{C1}}$
path 3	C1, $\overline{\text{C2}}$, C7∩C8, C5, $\overline{\text{C1}}$
path 4	C1, $\overline{\text{C3}}$, C7∩C8, C5, $\overline{\text{C1}}$
path 5	$\overline{\text{C1}}$

13.5.3 (e)

Using De Morgan's law, we get:

$$\text{C1 (C5}\cup\text{C6) } (\overline{\text{C3}}\cup\overline{\text{C4}}) \overline{\text{C1}} \cup \overline{\text{C1}}$$

This gives the following paths:

path 1	C1, C5, $\overline{\text{C3}}$, $\overline{\text{C1}}$
path 2	C1, C6, $\overline{\text{C3}}$, $\overline{\text{C1}}$
path 3	C1, C5, $\overline{\text{C4}}$, $\overline{\text{C1}}$
path 4	C1, C6, $\overline{\text{C4}}$, $\overline{\text{C1}}$
path 5	$\overline{\text{C1}}$

13.5.4 (a)

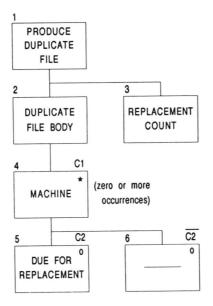

C1	End of file
C2	Due for replacement

13.5.4 (b)

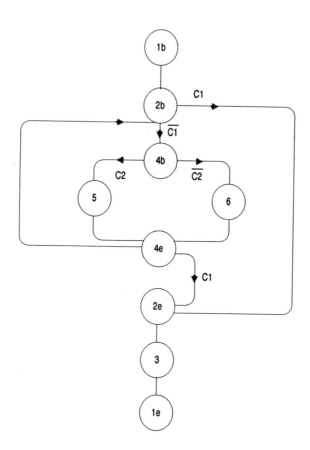

13.5.4 (c)

expr.1 : expr2
expr.2 : $\overline{C1}$ (expr.4) C1 ∪ C1
expr.4 : C2∪$\overline{C2}$

Hence

expr.1 : $\overline{C1}$ (C2∪$\overline{C2}$) C1 ∪ C1

13.5.4 (d)

path 1 $\overline{C1}$, C2, C1
path 2 $\overline{C1}$, $\overline{C2}$, C1
path 3   C1

13.5.4 (e)

path 1	Machine 1 due for replacement
	end of file
path 2	Machine 2 not due for replacement
	end of file
path 3	end of file

13.5.5 (a)

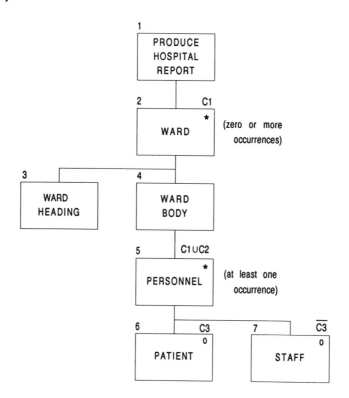

C1	End of file
C2	Change of ward
C3	Person is a patient

13.5.5 (b)

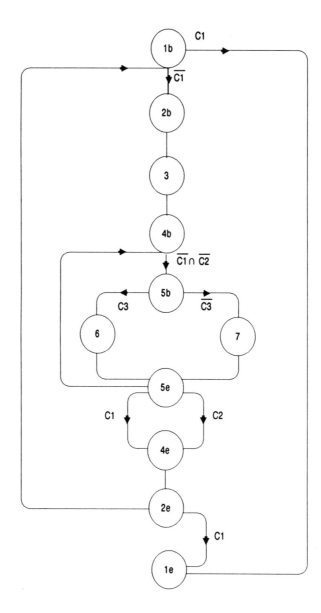

13.5.5 (c)

expr.1 : $\overline{C1}$ (expr.2) C1 ∪ C1
expr.2 : $\overline{expr.4}$
expr.4 : $\overline{(C1 \cup C2)}$ (expr.5) (C1 ∪ C2)
expr.5 : $C3 \cup \overline{C3}$

Hence

expr.1 : $\overline{C1}$ ($\overline{C1} \cap \overline{C2}$) ($C3 \cup \overline{C3}$) (C1 ∪ C2) C1 ∪ C1

13.5.5 (d)

path 1	$\overline{C1}$, $\overline{C1} \cap \overline{C2}$, C3, C1, C1
path 2	$\overline{C1}$, $\overline{C1} \cap \overline{C2}$, $\overline{C3}$, C1, C1
path 3	$\overline{C1}$, $\overline{C1} \cap \overline{C2}$, C3, C2, C1
path 4	$\overline{C1}$, $\overline{C1} \cap \overline{C2}$, $\overline{C3}$, C2, C1
path 5	C1

13.5.5 (e)

path 1	Ward A	J.Smith	patient
	end of file		
path 2	Ward A	I.Green	staff
	end of file		
path 3	Ward A	T.White	patient
	Ward B	F.Wise	patient
	end of file		
path 4	Ward A	M.Hall	staff
	Ward B	F.Young	staff
	end of file		
path 5	end of file		

Appendix B: An Invoice Printing Case Study

B.1 Objectives

To print invoices from a sales invoice file - see figure B.1. A single customer may have one invoice or one invoice with one or more extension invoices.

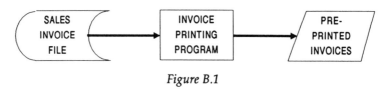

Figure B.1

B.2 Problem description

1. It is required to print invoices from a single sales invoice file. The file is structured such that there may be any number of sales detail records following each customer detail record. There may be more than one invoice to be printed per customer but, where it is necessary to print more than one invoice, the extension invoice(s) are identified by customer name only.

2. The sales details for each customer are in individual records (see SALES RECORD - figure B.2) following a record containing the customer's name and address (see CUSTOMER RECORD - figure B.3).

3. Each invoice can hold a maximum of 10 sales detail lines. If there are more than 10 sales details for a customer, extension invoices are produced. The extended invoices will contain a carried forward total, the extension invoices a brought forward total. The final invoice for a customer has a grand total. See figures B.4 and B.5 for samples of an extended first invoice and a final extension invoice.

```
┌─────────────────────────────────────────────────────┐
│                    SALES RECORD                      │
│  CUSTOMER NUMBER        4 digits                     │
│  PRODUCT DESCRIPTION    30 characters                │
│  PRICE                  6 digits                     │
│                         (including 2 dec. places)    │
└─────────────────────────────────────────────────────┘
```

Figure B.2

```
┌─────────────────────────────────────────────────────┐
│                    CUSTOMER RECORD                   │
│  CUSTOMER NUMBER        4 digits                     │
│  NAME                   20 characters                │
│  STREET                 20 characters                │
│  TOWN                   20 characters                │
│  COUNTY                 20 characters                │
└─────────────────────────────────────────────────────┘
```

Figure B.3

```
┌─────────────────────────────────────────────────────┐
│  P.J.PRENDERGAST LTD.,                               │
│  MARKET GARDENS,                                     │
│  APPLE TERRACE,                                      │
│  LONDON WC1 3AS                                      │
│                                                      │
│  30 BAGS GROW MORE MANURE            50.00           │
│  12 1KG BONE MEAL                    34.70           │
│  15 2KG BONE MEAL                    85.00           │
│  10 3KG BONE MEAL                    84.65           │
│  20 5KG BONE MEAL                   145.70           │
│  20 1KG BULB FIBRE                   74.42           │
│  24 2KG BULB FIBRE                  125.50           │
│  36 3KG BULB FIBRE                  240.70           │
│  18 4KG BULB FIBRE                  192.35           │
│  48 5KG BULB FIBRE                  405.63           │
│                                                      │
│              CARRIED FORWARD       1438.65           │
└─────────────────────────────────────────────────────┘
```

Figure B.4

```
P.J.PRENDERGAST LTD.,



                      BROUGHT  FORWARD    1438.65
9 DOZ MIXED TULIPS                         20.00
12 DOZ RED TULIPS                          15.00
20 DOZ BLUE TULIPS                         30.00
10 30KG PEAT                               25.00
20 50KG PEAT                               95.00




                        GRAND  TOTAL     1623.65
```

Figure B.5

Appendix C: A Label Production Case Study

C.1 Objectives

To produce adhesive label sets containing hospital patient identification information - see figure C.1. The number of individual labels per patient varies according to laboratory test categories.

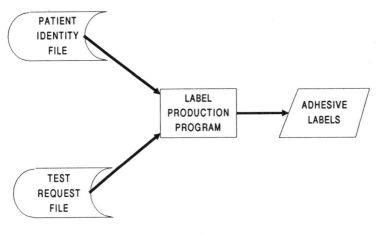

Figure C.1

C.2 Problem description

1. In a hospital system, a file (TEST REQUEST FILE) is created each day, containing records of patients due to enter hospital for laboratory tests. The records contain a patient number and test code, with just one record (that is, test) for each patient. The file is sorted into ascending order of patient number. Another sequential file (PATIENT IDENTITY FILE) is maintained, in patient number order, containing patient identification details (name, age etc.).

2. As both files are sorted into ascending order of patient number, we attempt to match records on the basis of this key field (see figures C.2 and C.3).
3. It is required to produce sets of adhesive labels, such that 3 labels are produced if the test code = 1; 4 labels if the test code = 2; 5 labels otherwise. In the event of patient identification details not being found for a particular test request record, a message is displayed to the computer operator (see figure C.4 for a sample set of labels).
4. The type of label available for printing is self-adhesive on continuous stationery backing, 3 across the page. The program should be easily modifiable to accommodate different types of labels.

```
                    PATIENT IDENTITY FILE
    PATIENT NUMBER          5 digits
    NAME                    15 characters
    AGE                     2 digits
    SEX                     1 character (M or F)
    CONSULTANT              15 characters
```

Figure C.2

```
                    TEST REQUEST FILE
    PATIENT NUMBER          5 digits
    TEST CODE               1 digit
```

Figure C.3

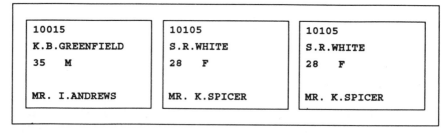

10015	10105	10105
K.B.GREENFIELD	S.R.WHITE	S.R.WHITE
35 M	28 F	28 F
MR. I.ANDREWS	MR. K.SPICER	MR. K.SPICER

Figure C.4

Appendix D: A Course File Completeness Case Study

D.1 Objectives

To read the course membership file and determine the extent of completeness
- see figure D.1

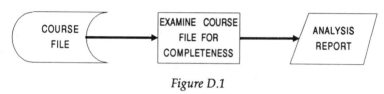

Figure D.1

D.2 Problem description

1. The file is sorted such that all records for a course are grouped together. A course may be complete (valid) or incomplete (invalid).
2. A complete course will consist of a header record (see HEADER RECORD - figure D.2); followed by a number of student description records (see DESCRIPTION RECORD - figure D.3); followed by a course end record (see END RECORD - figure D.4).
3. A course may be incomplete for three reasons:

      (a) the header record is missing;
or (b) the end record is missing;
or (c) the student count in the end record does not correspond with the number of student description records.

4. For a complete course only, it is required to print out details of each student (see figure D.5).
5. If a course is incomplete, only the first error detected is reported as a single line of print in the report (see figure D.5).
6. At the end of the report a summary line is produced showing the number of incomplete courses found (see figure D5).

```
┌─────────────────────────────────────────────────┐
│                  HEADER RECORD                    │
│  COURSE CODE         8 characters                 │
│  RECORD TYPE         1 character (= A)            │
└─────────────────────────────────────────────────┘
```

Figure D.2

```
┌─────────────────────────────────────────────────┐
│               DESCRIPTION RECORD                  │
│  COURSE CODE         8 characters                 │
│  RECORD TYPE         1 character (= B)            │
│  STUDENT NAME        15 characters                │
│  ADDRESS             24 characters                │
└─────────────────────────────────────────────────┘
```

Figure D.3

```
┌─────────────────────────────────────────────────┐
│                   END RECORD                      │
│  COURSE CODE         8 characters                 │
│  RECORD TYPE         1 character (= E)            │
│  STUDENT COUNT       3 digits                     │
└─────────────────────────────────────────────────┘
```

Figure D.4

```
┌───────────────────────────────────────────────────────┐
│  COURSE FILE - COMPLETENESS ANALYSIS     12-JAN-92     │
│  - - - - - - - - - - - - - - - - - - - - - - - - - -   │
│                                                         │
│   COURSE    STUDENT NAME      ADDRESS / COMMENT         │
│                                                         │
│  BSCASCIV  K.SHERROCKS       ROOM 2, BRYARS HALL        │
│  BSCASCIV  P.FORSTER         ROOM 29, MOUNTFORD BLDG    │
│                                                         │
│                                                         │
│  BSCASCII                    STUDENT COUNT INCORRECT    │
│                                                         │
│  BSCASCI                     HEADER RECORD MISSING      │
│                                                         │
│  HNDCSII                     END RECORD MISSING         │
│                                                         │
│          **   3 INVALID COURSES FOUND  **              │
└───────────────────────────────────────────────────────┘
```

Figure D.5

Appendix E: An Interactive System Case Study

E.1 Objectives

To allow the insertion of new contracts to, and the deletion of old contracts from, a microcomputer maintenance contract database. To allow certain interrogation facilities. See figure E.1.

Figure E.1

E.2 Problem description

1. Four facilities are required of the program:

   (a) insert new contract details (see screen layout INSERT NEW CON-TRACT - figure E.3);
   (b) delete cancelled contracts (see DELETE CANCELLED CONTRACT - figure E.4);
   (c) view or inspect the details of a given contract (see VIEW CONTRACT DETAILS - figure E.5);
   (d) list all contract details where the cost is high, that is, over £200 per annum (see LIST CONTRACT DETAILS - figure E.6).

   The selection of the required facilities is done by a simple menu (see MENU - figure E.2).
2. The only data validation, except by the user's visual inspection, is when attempts are made to access a contract that does not exist and when an invalid menu choice is made. In such cases an error message is displayed (see figures E.2, E.4 and E.5).

3. The simple database contains, for each contract, a contract number, a model description and the maintenance cost per annum. Facilities of the database management system, which can be incorporated into the program, include the ability to access directly any contract by reference to the contract number, and to find (or locate) all contracts with given attribute values (for example, model = 386SX, cost > £200) and return the number of records found.

```
 ┌─────────────────────────────────────────────────┐
 │                                                   │
 │      MICROCOMPUTER  MAINTENANCE  SYSTEM           │
 │      ------------------------------------         │
 │                    MENU                           │
 │                    ----                           │
 │                                                   │
 │      I.    Insert new contract(s)                 │
 │      D.    Delete cancelled contract(s)           │
 │      V.    View existing contract(s)              │
 │      L.    List high cost contracts               │
 │      E.    Exit from the system                   │
 │                                                   │
 │          Please enter I,D,V,L or E  [_]           │
 │                                                   │
 │  ****  INCORRECT ENTRY - PLEASE RE-ENTER  ****    │
 └─────────────────────────────────────────────────┘
```

Figure E.2

In figure E.2, the error message on the bottom line is displayed only after an incorrect entry and is cleared after the user has entered a new value. The user must eventually enter a correct value.

```
 ┌─────────────────────────────────────────────────┐
 │        MICROCOMPUTER  MAINTENANCE  SYSTEM         │
 │        ----------------------------------         │
 │               INSERT NEW CONTRACT                 │
 │               --------------------                │
 │                                                   │
 │        CONTRACT NO.  [_____]                     │
 │                                                   │
 │        MODEL  [_____]           │
 │                                                   │
 │        COST  [____.__]  P.A.                      │
 │                                                   │
 │  Please confirm that the above is correct (Y/N) [_]│
 │                                                   │
 │    Do you wish to enter another contract (Y/N) [_] │
 └─────────────────────────────────────────────────┘
```

Figure E.3

In figure E.3, the whole of the 'form' is displayed on the screen and the user is guided through it. After each response the cursor moves to the next position. The data are written to the database only if user confirmation response is Y. If the user elects to repeat the transaction, the entries on the form, but nothing else, are cleared.

```
        MICROCOMPUTER  MAINTENANCE  SYSTEM
        ■■■■■■■■■■■■■■■■■■■■■■■■■■■■■■■■■■■■
            DELETE  CANCELLED  CONTRACT
            ■■■■■■■■■■■■■■■■■■■■■■■■■■

        CONTRACT  NO.  [_____]

        MODEL   XXXXXXXXXXXXXXXXXXXXXXX

        COST  XXXX.XX

    Please  confirm  the  above  deletion  (Y/N)  [_]

 Do  you  wish  to  cancel  another  contract  (Y/N)  [_]

        ****  CONTRACT  DOES  NOT  EXIST  ****
```

Figure E.4

In figure E.4, the headings and the contract number prompt are displayed on a cleared screen. If the user enters a valid contract number, the contract details are displayed and then the user confirmation prompt. The record is deleted only if the confirmation response is Y. The repeat prompt is then displayed. For an invalid contract number, the error message is displayed and then the repeat prompt. If the user elects to delete another contract, the above process is repeated.

```
        MICROCOMPUTER  MAINTENANCE  SYSTEM
        ■■■■■■■■■■■■■■■■■■■■■■■■■■■■■■■■■■■■
            VIEW  CONTRACT  DETAILS
            ■■■■■■■■■■■■■■■■■■■■■■

        CONTRACT  NO.  [_____]

        MODEL   XXXXXXXXXXXXXXXXXXXXXXX

        COST  XXXX.XX

 Do  you  wish  to  view  another  contract  (Y/N)  [_]

        ****  CONTRACT  DOES  NOT  EXIST  ****
```

Figure E.5

The operation of the screen shown as figure E.5 is similar to the DELETE CANCELLED CONTRACT screen.

```
┌─────────────────────────────────────────────┐
│       MICROCOMPUTER  MAINTENANCE  SYSTEM      │
│       ■■■■■■■■■■■■■■■■■■■■■■■■■■■■■■■■■         │
│            LIST  CONTRACT  DETAILS            │
│            ■■■■■■■■■■■■■■■■■■■■■               │
│                                               │
│        CONTRACT  NO.  XXXXXX                  │
│                                               │
│        MODEL   XXXXXXXXXXXXXXXXXXXXXX          │
│                                               │
│        COST  XXXX.XX                          │
│                                               │
│     Please  press  any  key  to  continue  [_]│
└─────────────────────────────────────────────┘
```

Figure E.6

In figure E.6, the headings are displayed first. If there are no high cost contracts, the message

NO CONTRACTS FOUND

is displayed in the centre of the screen, and the prompt

PLEASE PRESS ANY KEY TO CONTINUE []

is displayed at the bottom of the screen. For each high cost contract, the details and prompt given in figure E.6 are displayed.

Appendix F: The Invoice Printing Case Study — a Solution

F.1 Stage 1 - the logical data structures

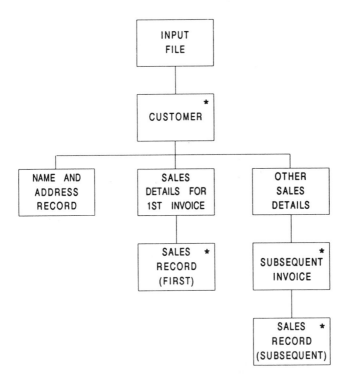

Figure F.1

In respect of the input file (see figure F.1), logically we know that the sales details for each customer may make up more than one invoice, of which the first has special significance in that it will contain full headings. We can reflect this, as shown above, by recognising that each customer has a sequence of a

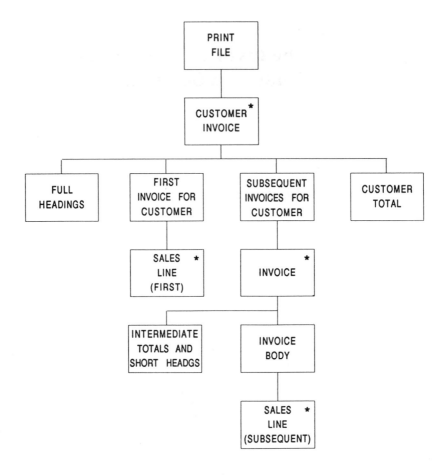

Figure F.2

name and address record, followed by the sales detail records, which make up the first invoice, followed by the sales detail records which make up any subsequent invoices.

The print file (see figure F.2) is also logically concerned with first and subsequent invoices, and also with final and intermediate totals. Note that the carried forward total at the end of an extended invoice, together with the name and brought forward total at the head of the extension invoice are grouped together as one component INTERMEDIATE TOTALS AND SHORT HEADGS.

F.2 Stage 2 - correspondences and program structure

The correspondences are:

INPUT FILE	corresponds to	PRINT FILE
CUSTOMER	corresponds to	CUSTOMER INVOICE
NAME AND ADDRESS RECORD	corresponds to	FULL HEADINGS
SALES DETAILS FOR 1ST INVOICE	corresponds to	FIRST INVOICE FOR CUSTOMER
OTHER SALES DETAILS	corresponds to	SUBSEQUENT INVOICES FOR CUSTOMER
SUBSEQUENT INVOICE	corresponds to	INVOICE
SALES RECORD (FIRST)	corresponds to	SALES LINE (FIRST)
SALES RECORD (SUBSEQUENT)	corresponds to	SALES LINE (SUBSEQUENT)

This leaves three components on the print file structure that have no corresponding components on the input file structure. Two of these are elementary components and as such will not affect the problem structure. The component INVOICE BODY is necessary only to avoid having two different component type parts at the same level. The program structure is shown in figure F.3.

F.3 Stage 3 - the condition and operation lists

There are four iterations in the program structure; this indicates four conditions, but we can use C2 in two places.

C1	Until end of input file
C2	Until change of customer or end of input file or expiration of line count (invoice full)
C3	Until change of customer or end of input file

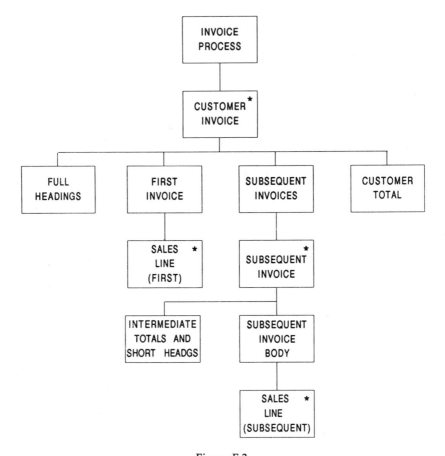

Figure F.3

1	Open files
2	Close files
3	Stop
4	Read an input file record
5	Print customer name and address at head of form
6	Print grand total
7	Print a sales detail line
8	Print stored customer name at head of form
9	Print brought forward total
10	Print carried forward total
11	Accumulate customer total
12	Store customer name (for short headings)
13	Initialise customer total (= 0)
14	Increment line count
15	Store customer number
16	Set line count = 0

F.4 Stage 4 - allocation of operations and conditions

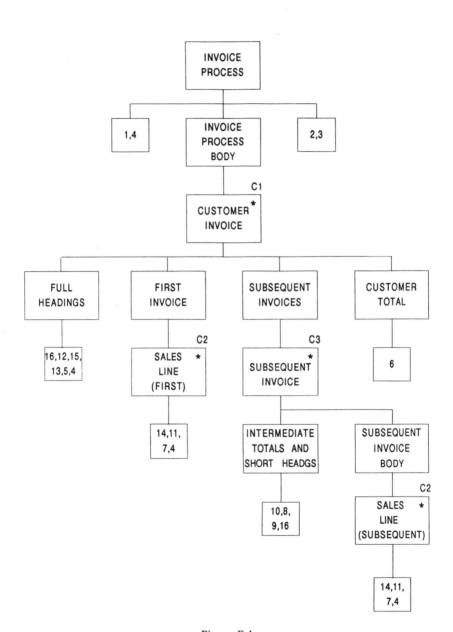

Figure F.4

F.5 Stage 5 - the schematic logic

```
INVOICE PROCESS SEQ
  DO 1   [Open files
  DO 4   [Read an input file record
  INVOICE PROCESS BODY ITER UNTIL C1 [end of input file
    CUSTOMER INVOICE SEQ
      FULL HEADINGS
        DO 16 [Set line count = 0
        DO 12 [Store customer name
        DO 15 [Store customer number
        DO 13 [Initialise customer total
        DO 5  [Print customer name and address at top of form
        DO 4  [Read an input file record
      FULL HEADINGS END
      FIRST INVOICE ITER UNTIL C2 [change of customer or end
                         of input file or expiration of line count
        SALES LINE (FIRST)
          DO 14 [Increment line count
          DO 11 [Accumulate customer total
          DO 7  [Print a sales detail line
          DO 4  [Read an input file record
        SALES LINE (FIRST) END
      FIRST INVOICE END
      SUBSEQUENT INVOICES ITER UNTIL C3 [change of customer
                                  or end of file
        SUBSEQUENT INVOICE SEQ
          INTERMEDIATE TOTALS AND SHORT HEADGS
            DO 10 [Print carried forward total
            DO 8  [Print stored customer name at head of form
            DO 9  [Print brought forward total
            DO 16 [Set line count = 0
          INTERMEDIATE TOTALS AND SHORT HEADGS END
          SUBSEQUENT INVOICE BODY ITER UNTIL C2 [change of
                              customer or end of input file or
                              expiration of line count
            SALES LINE (SUBSEQUENT)
              DO 14 [Increment line count
              DO 11 [Accumulate customer total
              DO 7  [Print a sales detail line
              DO 4  [Read an input file record
            SALES LINE (SUBSEQUENT) END
          SUBSEQUENT INVOICE BODY END
        SUBSEQUENT INVOICE END
      SUBSEQUENT INVOICES END
      CUSTOMER TOTAL
        DO 6  [Print grand total
      CUSTOMER TOTAL END
    CUSTOMER INVOICE END
  INVOICE PROCESS BODY END
  DO 2   [Close files
  DO 3   [Stop
INVOICE PROCESS END
```

Figure F.5

Appendix G: The Label Production Case Study — a Solution

G.1 Stage 1 - the logical data structures

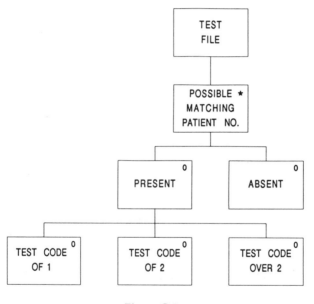

Figure G.1

The test file (see figure G.1) is logically an iteration of possible matching patient number that is either present or absent. If the patient number is present, then it is associated with a test code which has a choice (selection) of three pertinent values.

The patient identity file (see figure G.2) is also an iteration of possible matching patient number which is either present or absent.

Correspondences between the input files are easy to find, and follow the usual course for the merge or collate solution, giving the merged input file structure shown in figure G.3.

The output or label file (see figure G.4) is an iteration of label set each of
which, allowing for the last set, is an iteration of up to three labels.

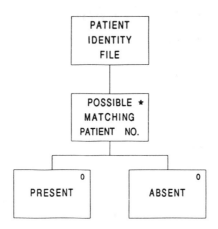

Figure G.2

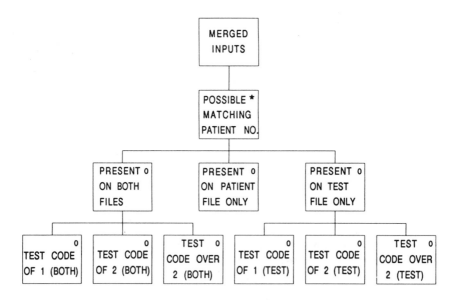

Figure G.3

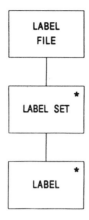

Figure G.4

G.2 Stage 2 - correspondences and program structure

The component MERGED INPUTS obviously corresponds to LABEL FILE, but there are no more correspondences. Since the labels for a particular patient may be contained within one label set (of 3) or spread over two or three label sets, the boundary of POSSIBLE MATCHING PATIENT NO. clashes with the boundary of LABEL SET. It is therefore impossible to produce a single program structure.

We solve the problem by designing two separate programs. Program 1 merges the two input files and produces an intermediate file of records containing the relevant label data (patient number, name etc.), with one record for each label. Program 2 then reads the intermediate file and produces labels, 3 up across the page.

(a) For program 1 the logical data structure for the intermediate file is shown in figure G.5.

We can now identify correspondences with the merged input file:

MERGED INPUTS   corresponds to INTERMEDIATE FILE

PRESENT ON BOTH   corresponds to MATCHED PATIENT NO.
FILES

TEST CODE OF 1 (BOTH) corresponds to THREE LABEL RECORDS

TEST CODE OF 2 (BOTH) corresponds to FOUR LABEL RECORDS

TEST CODE OF 3 (BOTH) corresponds to FIVE LABEL RECORDS

Thus the program structure is shown in figure G.6.

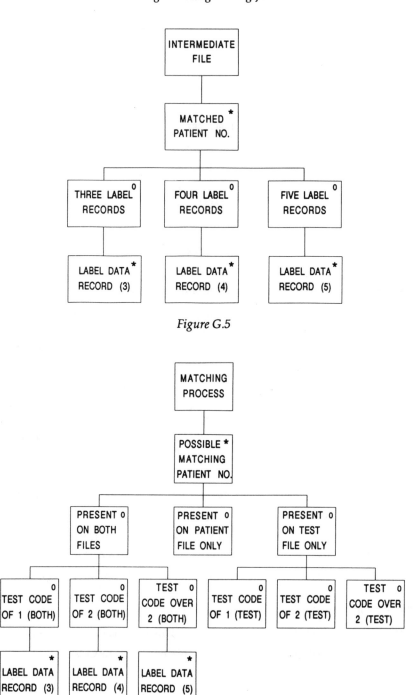

Figure G.5

Figure G.6

(b) *For program 2 the logical data structure for the intermediate file is given in figure G.7.*

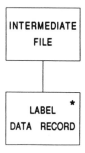

Figure G.7

Correspondences with the output file are now straightforward. LABEL FILE corresponds with INTERMEDIATE FILE and LABEL corresponds with LABEL DATA RECORD.

Thus the program structure is shown in figure G.8.

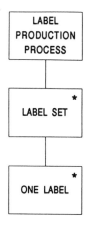

Figure G.8

After we have completed the design process for the two programs, we can use the technique of inversion to combine the two programs. This involves making one program a subprogram or procedure of the other.

G.3 Stage 3 - the condition and operation lists

(a) For program 1 - the matching process

Before listing the conditions and operations we note that each iteration of
LABEL DATA RECORD (N) is simply an iteration of N records (where N = 3
or 4 or 5). We can therefore remove each of these elementary components,
provided that we use elementary operations which write the appropriate
number of records.

C1	Until end of test request file
C2	If patient number of the test file = patient number of the patient identity file
C3	If patient number of the test file > patient number of the patient identity file
C4	If test code = 1
C5	If test code = 2
1	Open input files
2	Open intermediate file
3	Close input files
4	Close intermediate file
5	Stop
6	Read a test file record
7	Read a patient identity file record
8	Write 3 intermediate file records
9	Write 4 intermediate file records
10	Write 5 intermediate file records
11	Display error message

(b) For program 2 - the label production process

C1	Until end of intermediate file
C2	Until end of label set or end of intermediate file
1	Open intermediate file
2	Open label file
3	Close intermediate file
4	Close label file
5	Stop
6	Read an intermediate file record
7	Write a set of labels
8	Construct a label in set (indexed by label subscript)
9	Increment label subscript
10	Set label subscript = 1
11	Initialise a label set (space fill a label set area)

G.4 Stage 4 - allocation of conditions and operations

(a) Program 1 - the matching process

From the problem specification we note that each selection part of PRESENT ON TEST FILE ONLY generates the same error message. The selection is unnecessary and will therefore be omitted. Thus the program structure is as shown in figure G.9.

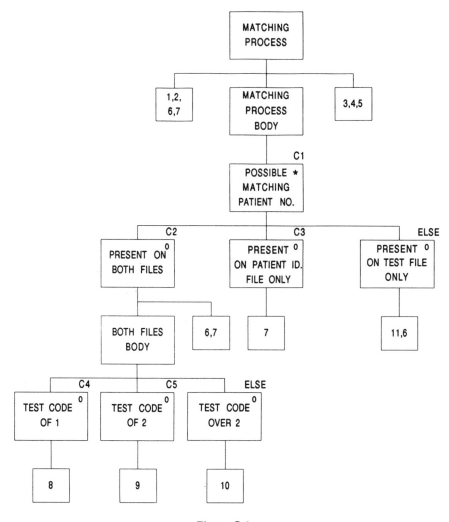

Figure G.9

(b) Program 2 - the label production process

See figure G.10.

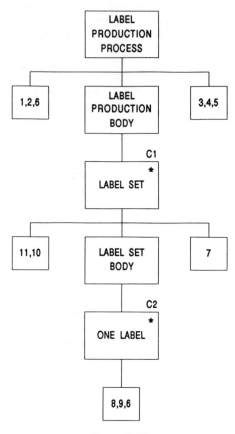

Figure G.10

G.5 Stage 5 - the schematic logic

See figures G.11 and G.12

```
MATCHING PROCESS SEQ
   DO 1    [Open input files
   DO 2    [Open intermediate file
   DO 6    [Read a test file record
   DO 7    [Read a patient identity file record
   MATCHING PROCESS BODY ITER UNTIL C1 [end of test request file
      POSSIBLE MATCHING PATIENT NO. SEL IF C2 [patient no. of the
             test file = patient no. of the patient identity file
         PRESENT ON BOTH FILES SEQ
            BOTH FILES BODY SEL IF C4 [test code = 1
               TEST CODE OF 1
                  DO 8   [Write 3 intermediate file records
               TEST CODE OF 1 END
            BOTH FILES BODY ELSE 1 IF C5 [test code = 2
               TEST CODE OF 2
                  DO 9   [Write 4 intermediate file records
               TEST CODE OF 2 END
            BOTH FILES BODY ELSE 2
               TEST CODE OVER 2
                  DO 10 [Write 5 intermediate file records
               TEST CODE OVER 2 END
            BOTH FILES BODY END
            DO 6    [Read a test file record
            DO 7    [Read a patient identity file record
         PRESENT ON BOTH FILES END
      POSSIBLE MATCHING PATIENT NO. ELSE 1 IF C3 [patient no. of
         the test file > patient no. of the patient identity file
         PRESENT ON PATIENT ID FILE ONLY
            DO 7    [Read a patient identity file record
         PRESENT ON PATIENT ID FILE ONLY
      POSSIBLE MATCHING PATIENT NO. ELSE 2
         PRESENT ON TEST FILE ONLY
            DO 11 [Display error message
            DO 6    [Read a test file record
         PRESENT ON TEST FILE ONLY END
      POSSIBLE MATCHING PATIENT NO. END
   MATCHING PROCESS BODY END
   DO 3    [Close input files
   DO 4    [Close intermediate file
   DO 5    [Stop
MATCHING PROCESS END
```

Figure G.11

```
LABEL PRODUCTION PROCESS SEQ
  DO 1   [Open intermediate file
  DO 2   [Open label file
  DO 6   [Read an intermediate file record
  LABEL PRODUCTION BODY ITER UNTIL C1 [end of intermediate file
    LABEL SET SEQ
      DO 11 [Initialise a label set (space fill a label set
             area)
      DO 10 [Set label subscript = 1
      LABEL SET BODY ITER UNTIL C2 [end of label set or end of
                                    intermediate file
        ONE LABEL
          DO 8   [Construct a label in set (label subscript)
          DO 9   [Increment label subscript
          DO 6   [Read an intermediate file record
        ONE LABEL END
      LABEL SET BODY END
      DO 7   [Write a set of labels
    LABEL SET END
  LABEL PRODUCTION BODY END
  DO 3   [Close intermediate file
  DO 4   [Close label file
  DO 5   [Stop
LABEL PRODUCTION PROCESS END
```

Figure G.12

G.6 Stage 6 - applying the technique of inversion

We shall choose to make the label production process a subprogram of the matching program. This means observing the following when implementing our design in the target language.

(a) For the main program (program 1)

We code

2	Open intermediate file

by initialising an intermediate file status indicator.

We code

8, 9 and 10	Write intermediate file records

by calling the subprogram N times and passing the two parameters: the intermediate file record and the intermediate file status indicator.

We code

4	Close intermediate file

by calling the subprogram with the intermediate file status indicator set to 'end of file'.

(b) For the subprogram (program 2)

At the start of the subprogram we include code to implement the control passing mechanism for logical reads.

We code

1	Open intermediate file

and the first occurrence of

6	Read an intermediate file record

by nothing.

We code the other occurrence of

6	Read an intermediate file record

by setting the entry status indicator to a value of 2, indicating which occurrence of the 'read' it is, then exiting from the subprogram, then inserting an entry-point label.

We code

3	Close intermediate file record

by nothing.

We code

5	Stop

by code to exit from the subprogram.

Appendix H: The Course File Completeness Case Study — a Solution

H.1 Stage 1 - the logical data structures

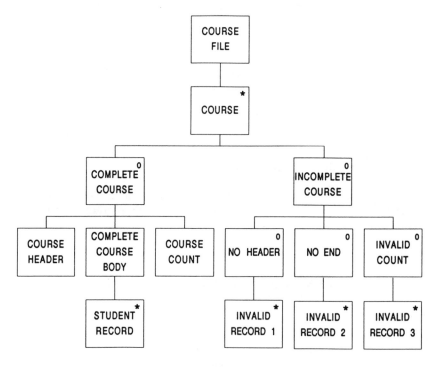

Figure H.1

The course file (figure H.1) is an iteration of course, each of which may be regarded as either complete (valid) or incomplete (invalid). A complete course is a sequence of a header, followed by a body (which is an iteration of student record), followed by an end record. The incomplete course is a selection of the causes of incompleteness, because each cause gives rise to a different error

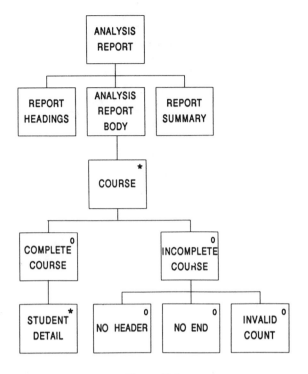

Figure H.2

message (that is, no header or no end record or invalid count of students). Each type of incomplete course is an iteration of invalid record

The report (figure H.2) has headings followed by the main body followed by the summary line. The report body is an iteration of course, each of which may be complete or incomplete. The former is simply an iteration of student detail; the latter a choice of error reasons (messages).

H.2 Stage 2 - correspondences and program structure

There are eight points of correspondence:

COURSE FILE	corresponds to ANALYSIS REPORT
COURSE	corresponds to COURSE
COMPLETE COURSE	corresponds to COMPLETE COURSE
INCOMPLETE COURSE	corresponds to INCOMPLETE COURSE
STUDENT RECORD	corresponds to STUDENT DETAIL
NO HEADER	corresponds to NO HEADER
NO END	corresponds to NO END
INVALID COUNT	corresponds to INVALID COUNT

The resultant program structure is shown in figure H.3.

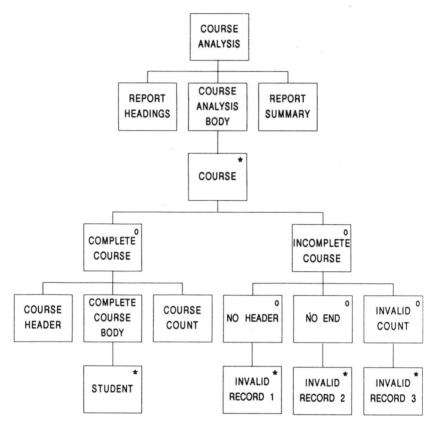

Figure H.3

H.3 Stage 3 - the condition and operation lists

C1	Until end of course file
C2	If a complete course !!!
C3	Until course end record
C4	If error 'header record missing'
C5	If error 'end record missing'
C6	Until change of course or end of file

1	Open files
2	Close files
3	Stop
4	Read a course file record
5	Print analysis headings
6	Print a student's details
7	Print error line 'student count incorrect'
8	Print error line 'header record missing'
9	Print error line 'end record missing'
10	Print summary
11	Increment student record count
12	Increment incomplete course count
13	Initialise student record count
14	Initialise incomplete course count
15	Store course code

H.4 Stage 4 - allocation of conditions and operations

Condition C2 cannot be appropriately implemented, so we recognise a backtracking problem. We will continue with the allocation, which leads to the following revised program structure shown in figure H.4

H.5 Stage 5 - the schematic logic

Having established a backtracking solution, the selection COURSE BODY becomes a POSIT/ADMIT construct and QUITs are introduced in the POSIT component when causes for incompleteness are recognised. The intolerable side effect of printing a student's details (if the course turns out to be incomplete) is dealt with by postponing the printing. Operation 6 becomes

6	Store a student's details in a temporary file

and a new operation must be introduced to accommodate the printing after all QUITs have been passed:

16	Print all student details from the temporary file

To support operations 6 and 16 we also need:

17	Initialise temporary file

The revised schematic logic is shown in figure H.5.

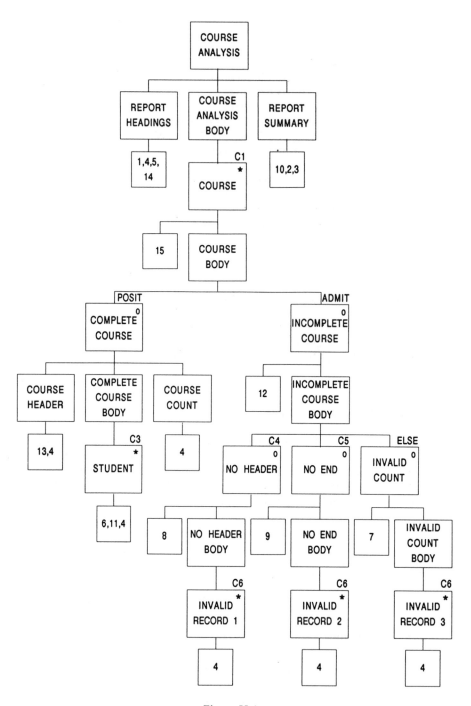

Figure H.4

```
COURSE ANALYSIS SEQ
  REPORT HEADINGS
    DO 1   [Open files
    DO 4   [Read a course file record
    DO 5   [Print analysis headings
    DO 14  [Initialise incomplete course count
  REPORT HEADINGS END
  COURSE ANALYSIS BODY ITER UNTIL C1 [end of course file
    COURSE SEQ
      DO 15 [Store course code
      COURSE BODY POSIT (Complete course)
        DO 17 [Initialise temporary file
        COMPLETE COURSE SEQ
          COURSE HEADER
            QUIT COURSE BODY POSIT IF C7 [not a course header
            DO 13 [Initialise student record count
            DC 4  [Read a course file record
            QUIT COURSE BODY POSIT IF C8 [not the same course
                                                 or end of file
          COURSE HEADER END
          COMPLETE COURSE BODY ITER UNTIL C3 [course end record
            STUDENT
              DO 6  [Store a student's details in temp. file
              DO 11 [Increment student record count
              DO 4  [Read a course file record
              QUIT COURSE BODY POSIT IF C8 [not the same course
                                                 or end of file
            STUDENT END
          COMPLETE COURSE BODY END
          COURSE COUNT
            QUIT COURSE BODY POSIT IF C9 [computed count <> end
                                             record count
            DO 16 [Print all student details from temp. file
            DO 4  [Read a course file record
          COURSE COUNT END
        COMPLETE COURSE END
      COURSE BODY ADMIT (Incomplete course)
        INCOMPLETE COURSE SEQ
          DO 12 [Increment incomplete course count
          INCOMPLETE COURSE BODY SEL IF C4 [error 'heading
                                             record missing'
            NO HEADER SEQ
              DO 8  [Print error line 'header record missing'
              NO HEADER BODY ITER UNTIL C6 [change of course or
                                             end of file
                INVALID RECORD 1
                  DO 4  [Read a course file record
                INVALID RECORD 1 END
              NO HEADER BODY END
            NO HEADER END
          INCOMPLETE COURSE BODY ELSE 1 IF C5 [error 'end
                                             record missing'
            NO END SEQ
              DO 9  [Print error line 'end record missing'
```

Figure H.5 above and overleaf

```
                  NO END BODY ITER UNTIL C6 [change of course or
                                              end of file
                  INVALID RECORD 2
                    DO 4   [Read a course file record
                  INVALID RECORD 2 END
                NO END BODY END
              NO END END
            INCOMPLETE COURSE BODY ELSE 2
              INVALID COUNT SEQ
                DO 7   [Print error line 'student count incorrect'
                INVALID COUNT BODY ITER UNTIL C6 [change of
                                          course or end of file
                  INVALID RECORD 3
                    DO 4   [Read a course file record
                  INVALID RECORD 3 END
                INVALID COUNT BODY END
              INVALID COUNT END
            INCOMPLETE COURSE BODY END
          INCOMPLETE COURSE END
        COURSE BODY END
      COURSE END
    COURSE ANALYSIS BODY END
    REPORT SUMMARY
      DO 10 [Print summary
      DO 2   [Close files
      DO 3   [Stop
    REPORT SUMMARY END
  COURSE ANALYSIS END
```

Appendix I: The Interactive System Case Study — a Solution

As we develop the data structure for the menu screen, it becomes apparent that we can best proceed by designing five small processes: a menu driver as the main program and four separate subprograms for the facilities insert, delete, view and list. Furthermore, the simple database, with its direct access facilities, will not influence our design. This means that the structure of each screen becomes the appropriate subprogram structure. The solution is therefore presented in the form of five program structures with allocated operations and conditions.

The program structure for the MENU driver process is first given - see figure I.1.

The condition and operation list is:

C1	Until user chooses to exit (note that this is implemented by allocating a QUIT from iteration to the component EXIT)
C2	Until a valid response
C3	If an insert request
C4	If a deletion request
C5	If a view request
C6	If a list request
1	Initialise (open) database
2	Reset (close) database
3	Stop
4	Display headings on clear screen
5	Display menu lines
6	Display selection prompt
7	Accept menu choice
8	Display error message
9	Clear error message from screen
10	Call insert requests procedure
11	Call deletion requests procedure
12	Call view requests procedure
13	Call list request procedure

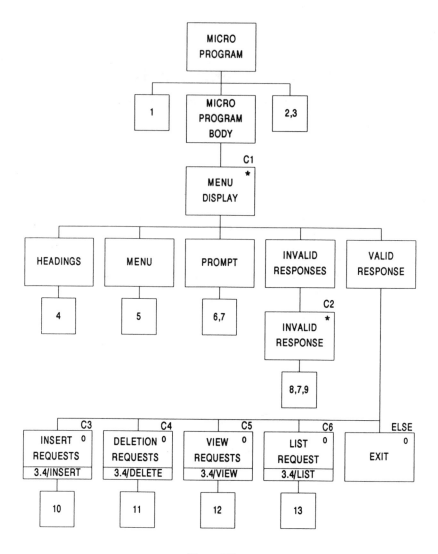

Figure I.1

Next we show the INSERT REQUESTS procedure - see figure I.2.
The condition and operation list is:

C11	Until user no longer requires this option (note that this is implemented by allocating a conditional QUIT from iteration to the component REPEAT RESPONSE after operation 17)
C12	If user confirmation = 'Y'

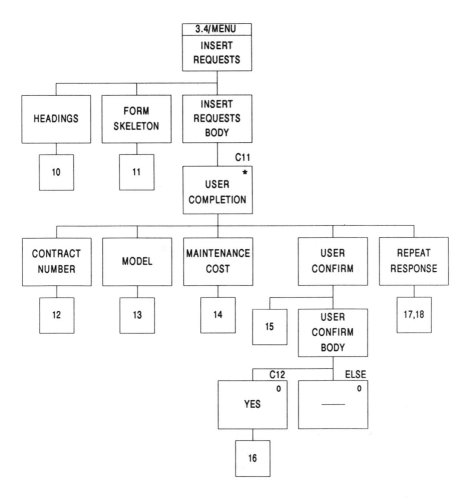

Figure I.2

10	Display headings on clear screen
11	Display insertion 'form' skeleton
12	Accept contract number
13	Accept model
14	Accept maintenance cost
15	Accept user confirmation
16	Write new data to database
17	Accept repeat response
18	Clear form entries

Next we show the DELETION REQUESTS procedure - see figure I.3.

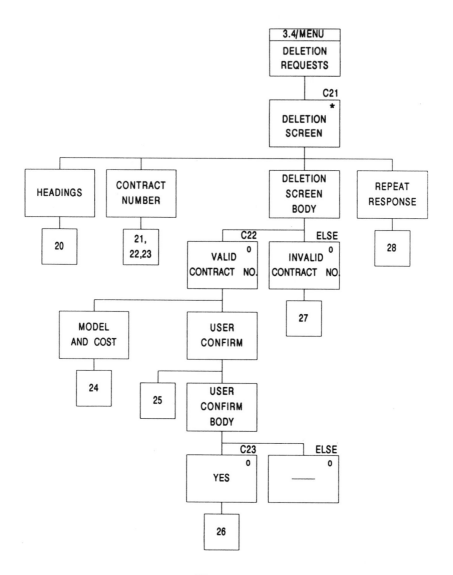

Figure I.3

The condition and operation list is:

C21	Until user no longer requires this option (note that this is implemented by allocating a conditional QUIT from iteration to the component REPEAT RESPONSE after operation 28)
C22	If contract number found in database
C23	If user confirmation = 'Y'
20	Clear screen and display headings
21	Display contract no. prompt
22	Accept contract number
23	Attempt to retrieve contract details
24	Display model and cost
25	Display prompt and accept user confirmation
26	Delete contract from database
27	Display error message
28	Display prompt and accept repeat request

Next we show the VIEW REQUESTS procedure - see figure I.4.

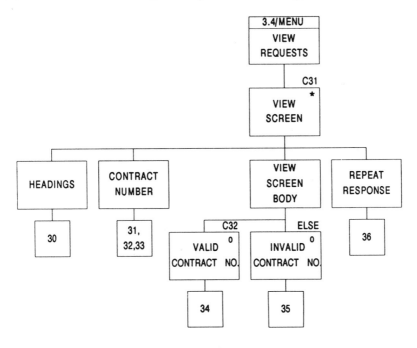

Figure I.4

The condition and operation list is:

> C31 Until user no longer requires this option (note that
>   this is implemented by allocating a conditional
>   QUIT from iteration to the component REPEAT
>   RESPONSE after operation 36)
> C32 If contract number found in database
>
> 30   Clear screen and display headings
> 31   Display contract no. prompt
> 32   Accept contract number
> 33   Attempt to retrieve contract details
> 34   Display model and cost
> 35   Display error message
> 36   Display prompt and accept repeat response

Finally, we show the LIST REQUEST procedure - see figure I.5.

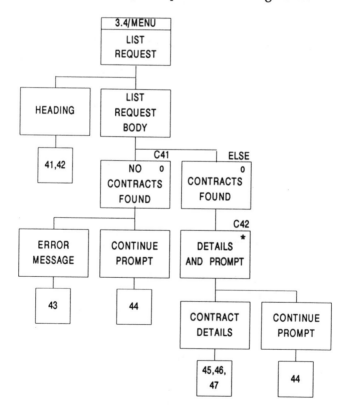

Figure I.5

The condition and operation list is:

C41	If no contracts found
C42	Until the count of records to be displayed is zero
41	Display headings
42	Find all contracts where cost is 'high'; store number found in counter
43	Display 'none found'
44	Display prompt and accept user continue signal
45	Retrieve the next record found
46	Clear screen body and display contract details
47	Decrement count of records

Appendix J: Complete Programs for the Inversion Example (Chapter 9)

```
IDENTIFICATION DIVISION.
**** Program to produce an intermediate file ****
**** from the student file ****
PROGRAM-ID. STUDRP.
ENVIRONMENT DIVISION.
INPUT-OUTPUT SECTION.
FILE-CONTROL.
    SELECT STUDENT-FILE ASSIGN TO "STUDENT.SEQ".
DATA DIVISION.
FILE SECTION.
FD  STUDENT-FILE.
01  STUDENT-FILE-REC.
    03 COURSE-CODE      PIC X(8).
    03 NAME             PIC X(20).
    03 MARK             PIC 999.
WORKING-STORAGE SECTION.
77  INTER-EOF           PIC 9.
77  COURSE-TOT          PIC S9(5).
77  STORED-COURSE       PIC X(8).
01  DETAIL-RECORD.
    03 D-REC-TYPE        PIC X.
    03 D-REC-DATA.
       05 D-COURSE       PIC X(10).
       05 D-NAME         PIC X(22).
       05 D-MARK         PIC -(5)9.
01  TOTAL-RECORD.
    03 T-REC-TYPE        PIC X.
    03 T-REC-DATA.
       05 T-COURSE       PIC X(10).
       05 FILLER         PIC X(22) VALUE "TOTAL".
       05 T-TOTAL        PIC -(5)9.
01  NULL-RECORD          PIC X(40) VALUE LOW-VALUES.
PROCEDURE DIVISION.
PROD-INTER-FILE-SEQ.
    OPEN INPUT STUDENT-FILE.
    MOVE 0 TO INTER-EOF.
    READ STUDENT-FILE
        AT END MOVE HIGH-VALUES TO COURSE-CODE.
PROD-INTER-FILE-BODY-ITER.
    IF COURSE-CODE = HIGH-VALUES
        GO TO PROD-INTER-FILE-BODY-END.
COURSE-SEQ.
    MOVE 0 TO COURSE-TOT.
    MOVE COURSE-CODE TO STORED-COURSE.
```

```
COURSE-BODY-ITER.
    IF (STORED-COURSE NOT = COURSE-CODE) OR
       (COURSE-CODE = HIGH-VALUES)
        GO TO COURSE-BODY-END.
MARK-TO-LINE.
    MOVE "D" TO D-REC-TYPE.
    MOVE COURSE-CODE TO D-COURSE.
    MOVE NAME TO D-NAME.
    MOVE MARK TO D-MARK.
    CALL REP-SR USING INTER-EOF DETAIL-RECORD.
    ADD MARK TO COURSE-TOT.
    READ STUDENT-FILE
        AT END MOVE HIGH-VALUES TO COURSE-CODE.
MARK-TO-LINE-END.
    GO TO COURSE-BODY-ITER.
COURSE-BODY-END.
COURSE-TOTAL.
    MOVE "T" TO T-REC-TYPE.
    MOVE STORED-COURSE TO T-COURSE.
    MOVE COURSE-TOT TO T-TOTAL.
    CALL REP-SR USING INTER-EOF TOTAL-RÉCORD.
COURSE-TOTAL-END.
COURSE-END.
    GO TO PROD-INTER-FILE-BODY-ITER.
PROD-INTER-FILE-BODY-END.
    CLOSE STUDENT-FILE.
    MOVE 1 TO INTER-EOF.
    CALL REP-SR USING INTER-EOF NULL-RECORD.
    STOP RUN.
PROD-INTER-FILE-END.


IDENTIFICATION DIVISION.
**** Subprogram to produce report ****
**** from the intermediate file ****
PROGRAM-ID. REP-SR.
ENVIRONMENT DIVISION.
CONFIGURATION SECTION.
SPECIAL-NAMES. CHANNEL (1) IS HEAD-OF-FORM.
INPUT-OUTPUT SECTION.
FILE-CONTROL.
    SELECT MARKS-FILE ASSIGN TO "MARKS.SEQ".
DATA DIVISION.
FILE SECTION.
FD  MARKS-FILE.
01  MARKS-FILE-REC          PIC X(80).
LINKAGE SECTION.
01  DATA-RECORD.
    03 L-REC-TYPE           PIC X.
    03 L-REC-DATA           PIC X(38).
77  INTER-EOF               PIC 9.
WORKING-STORAGE SECTION.
77  ENTRY-STATUS            PIC 9       VALUE 1.
77  LINE-COUNT              PIC 99.
01  HEADINGS-REC            PIC X(40) VALUE
    "STUDENT MARKS FOR ALL FULL-TIME COURSES".
```

```
PROCEDURE DIVISION USING INTER-EOF DATA-RECORD.
PROD-REPORT-SEQ.
    GO TO ENTRY-1 ENTRY-2 DEPENDING ON ENTRY-STATUS.
ENTRY-1.
    OPEN OUTPUT MARKS-FILE.
PROD-REPORT-BODY-ITER.
    IF INTER-EOF = 1
        GO TO PROD-REPORT-BODY-END.
PAGE-SEQ.
PAGE-HEADING.
    WRITE MARKS-FILE-REC FROM HEADINGS-REC AFTER HEAD-OF-FORM.
    WRITE MARKS-FILE-REC FROM SPACES AFTER 2.
    MOVE 0 TO LINE-COUNT.
PAGE-HEADING-END.
PAGE-BODY-ITER.
    IF INTER-EOF = 1 OR LINE-COUNT > 20
        GO TO PAGE-BODY-END.
LINE-SEQ.
LINE-BODY-SEL.
    IF L-REC-TYPE = "D"
        NEXT SENTENCE
    ELSE
        GO TO LINE-BODY-ELSE-1.
DETAIL.
    WRITE MARKS-FILE-REC FROM L-REC-DATA AFTER 1.
    ADD 1 TO LINE-COUNT.
DETAIL-END.
    GO TO LINE-BODY-END.
LINE-BODY-ELSE-1.
TOTAL.
    WRITE MARKS-FILE-REC FROM L-REC-DATA AFTER 2.
    WRITE MARKS-FILE-REC FROM SPACES AFTER 2.
    ADD 4 TO LINE-COUNT.
TOTAL-END.
LINE-BODY-END.
    MOVE 2 TO ENTRY-STATUS.
    EXIT PROGRAM.
ENTRY-2.
LINE-END.
    GO TO PAGE-BODY-ITER.
PAGE-BODY-END.
PAGE-END.
    GO TO PROD-REPORT-BODY-ITER.
PROD-REPORT-BODY-END.
    CLOSE MARKS-FILE.
    EXIT PROGRAM.
PROD-REPORT-END.
```

Figure J.1

```
PROGRAM Marks (student_file, report_file) ;

TYPE
   course_string   = PACKED ARRAY [1..8] OF char ;
   student_rectype = RECORD
                        course_code : course_string ;
                        name        : PACKED ARRAY [1..20]
                                         OF char ;
                        mark        : 0..100 ;
                     END ;
VAR
   entry_status    : 1..2 ;
   inter_eof       : boolean ;
   line_count      : integer ;
   stored_course   : course_string ;
   course_total    : integer ;
   rectype         : char ;
   student_rec     : student_rectype ;
   student_file    : FILE OF student_rectype ;
   report_file     : text ;

PROCEDURE Reportsr ;

LABEL
   10,20,9999 ;

CONST
   page_headings   = 'STUDENT MARKS FOR ALL FULL-TIME COURSES' ;

BEGIN
(* produce report seq *)
   IF entry_status = 1 THEN GOTO 10
   ELSE IF entry_status = 2 THEN GOTO 20 ;
   10:
   Rewrite (report_file) ;
   (* produce report body iter *)
   WHILE NOT inter_eof DO
     BEGIN
     (* page seq *)
       (* page heading *)
         Page (report_file) ;
         Writeln (report_file, page_headings:39) ;
         Writeln (report_file) ;
         Writeln (report_file) ;
         line_count := 0 ;
       (* page heading end *)
       (* page body iter *)
       WHILE NOT (inter_eof OR (line_count > 20)) DO
         BEGIN
         (* line seq *)
           (* line body sel *)
           IF rectype = 'D' THEN
             BEGIN
             (* detail *)
               WITH student_rec DO
                 Writeln (report_file, course_code:10,
```

```
                    name:22, mark:6) ;
               line_count := line_count + 1 ;
             (* detail end *)
             END
           (* line body else 1 *)
           ELSE
             BEGIN
             (* total *)
               Writeln (report_file) ;
               Writeln (report_file, stored_course:10,
                 'total':22, course_total:6) ;
               Writeln (report_file) ;
               Writeln (report_file) ;
               line_count := line_count + 4 ;
             (* total end *)
             END ;
           (* line body end *)
           entry_status := 2 ;
           GOTO 9999 ;
           20:
         (* line end *)
         END ;
      (* page body end *)
    (* page end *)
    END ;
  (* produce report body end *)
  9999:
(* produce report end *)
END ;

BEGIN
(* produce intermediate file seq *)
  entry_status := 1 ;
  Reset (student_file) ;
  inter_eof := FALSE ;
  Read (student_file, student_rec) ;
  WITH student_rec DO
  (* produce intermediate file body iter *)
  WHILE NOT (course_code = 'ZZZZ    ') DO
    BEGIN
    (* course seq *)
      course_total := 0 ;
      stored_course := course_code ;
      (* course body iter *)
      WHILE NOT ((stored_course <> course_code) OR
        (course_code = 'ZZZZ    ')) DO
        BEGIN
        (* mark to line *)
          rectype := 'D' ;
          Reportsr ;
          course_total := course_total + mark ;
          Read (student_file, student_rec) ;
        (* mark to line end *)
        END ;
      (* course body end *)
      (* course total *)
```

```
        rectype := 'T' ;
        Reportsr ;
      (* course total end *)
    (* course end *)
   END ;
  (* produce intermediate file body end *)
  inter_eof := TRUE ;
  Reportsr ;
 (* produce intermediate file end *)
END.
```

Figure J.2